"In this beguiling reflection of the complicated path to becoming a gay dad in China in the 1990s, Peter Rupert Lighte describes a passionate longing for children and the extraordinary machinations necessary to fulfill it. His writing, bubbly and exuberant, belies the seriousness of his undertaking, which required remarkable tact and social sensitivity, even diplomacy. This is a book full of love stories, a testament to ecstatic generosity."

—**Andrew Solomon**, author of *Far & Away* and professor of Clinical Medical Psychology, Columbia University

"In Peter Rupert Lighte's quest to adopt two girls from China, the possibility of failure and reversals marched in parallel with an almost romantic but always unwavering determination to raise a family with his husband. This emotionally gripping and occasionally nerve-wracking account is a striking achievement."

—**May Holdsworth**, author of *Crime, Justice and Punishment in Colonial Hong Kong*

"This extraordinary tale—an adventure through a maze of emotion—is groundbreaking in many ways. Social and cultural barriers are negotiated, political and bureaucratic obstacles confronted, and formidable meals devoured. It's a unique story, beautifully told, with two charming children and their two doting fathers."

—**Kate Adie**, BBC news correspondent and author of *Nobody's Child*

"An epic history of family as the creation of a love that moves mountains. Peter Rupert Lighte has given us a rare masterpiece of deep, eloquent courage. Every family of every kind needs his truth-bearing witness."

—**Sarah Jones Nelson**, advisor to the Vatican

"Peter Lighte's journey to fatherhood offers a tale highly specific but also universal, about the search for love and family and redemption, told with candidness and a sharp wit."
—**Shai Oster**, Pulitzer Prize–winning journalist

STRAIGHT THROUGH THE LABYRINTH

Becoming a Gay Father in China

PETER RUPERT LIGHTE

Foreword by Andrew Moravcsik and
Anne-Marie Slaughter

Acausal Books
Princeton, New Jersey

Published by: Acausal Books
27 Haslet Avenue
Princeton, NJ 08540
www.acausalbooks.com

Editors: Ellen Kleiner and David Groff
Book design and production: Janice St. Marie
Cover design: A Bomb in a Bull
Calligraphy: Peter Rupert Lighte

First Edition

Copyright © 2022 by Peter Rupert Lighte

Proceeds from the sale of this book benefit Capital Harmony Works, an organization that empowers young people in Trenton, New Jersey, to transform their lives and society through shared musical experiences.

Printed in the United States of America

Publisher's Cataloging-in-Publication Data

Names: Lighte, Peter Rupert, author. | Moravcsik, Andrew, writer of foreword. | Slaughter, Anne-Marie, 1958 - writer of foreword.

Title: Straight through the labyrinth : becoming a gay father in China / Peter Rupert Lighte ; foreword by Andrew Moravcsik and Anne-Marie Slaughter.

Description: First edition. | Princeton, New Jersey : Acausal Books, 2022.

Identifiers: ISBN: 978-0-9912529-0-9 (paperback) | 978-0-9912529-1-6 (ebook) | LCCN: 2021924208

Subjects: LCSH: Gay adoption--Law and legislation--China--Hong Kong. | Gay parents--Legal status, laws, etc.--China--Hong Kong. | Gay-parent families--China--Hong Kong. | Gay men--Social conditions--China--Hong Kong. | Gay men--Legal status, laws, etc.--China--Hong Kong.

Classification: LCC: HV875.72.C6 L54 2022 | DDC: 362.734/0895125--dc23

1 3 5 7 9 10 8 6 4 2

For Julian Grant,
father of my children,
and
to celebrate the memory of the Honorable Xu Liugen,
godfather of our family, and Larry Lipton,
playmate like no other, well into our sunset years

A certain man once lost a diamond cuff-link in the wide blue sea, and twenty years later, on the exact day, a Friday apparently, he was eating a large fish—but there was no diamond inside. That's what I like about coincidence.

—VLADIMIR NABOKOV, *LAUGHTER IN THE DARK*

CONTENTS

FOREWORD

ABOUT A DECADE AGO, after returning from a sabbatical year in Shanghai, we threw a small holiday party. Anne-Marie's parents were visiting from Virginia. Peter Lighte and his husband Julian Grant, who had also recently left China to settle in Princeton, New Jersey, came and were their charming and dashing selves. After we sent them off into the frosty December night with warm good-byes, the four of us settled back around the fire for a last drink. Mom and Dad commented on what a remarkable coincidence it was that both Peter and Julian had been in China and that each had adopted a daughter there who was now attending school in Princeton. It took us a moment to sort out what they meant before we realized that they had no inkling that Peter and Julian were a couple. They had simply assumed that the respective spouses were both absent that evening. We explained, and all laughed, although with some incredulity on our part.

This brief misunderstanding illustrates how far mores and presuppositions have shifted in recent decades. For Anne-Marie's father and others who graduated from college in 1953, two men married to one another and raising a family could only have been some type of (probably dystopian) fantasy fiction. For Peter and his collegiate contemporaries two decades later, the cultural upheavals of the 1960s had opened doors to new pathways through life—even if it would take decades for their destinations to become fully clear. Today, we accept same-sex couples with children as the new normal.

This anecdote also captures the arc of Peter's life, so movingly and vividly told in *Straight Through the Labyrinth*, which traces this transformation as he lived it, relating how he became a family,

11

adopting his daughters Hattie and Tillie in China. Yet even he initially struggled to tell his own story of transformation. The first draft of the book focused primarily on the daughters rather than on the father's life circumstances or pioneering the adoption of children as a gay man. Only the final version reveals that Peter was a lonely child of a fractured set of marriages who only gradually came to realize that "life did not have to simply happen to me, that I could affect the narrative of my own future." Ultimately, he did let us into his life and soul—relating with honesty and passion what this passage meant to him.

And what a story he has written! Peter's is a life in which he adopted a country and a culture just as determinedly as he would eventually adopt an identity and two daughters. He fell in love with China as an undergraduate and then gained a PhD in East Asian Studies at Princeton, becoming what he terms (with typically disingenuous self-deprecation) a "calligraphy bore." He taught Asian history at Oberlin, Middlebury, and the University of Santa Clara and German philosophy at Princeton—only then to be offered a chance to open the Beijing office for a major international bank with the promise that he could be a "renaissance banker." Subsequently realizing "there was no need to remove Confucius to make room for corporate finance," he left academia.

Peter is a man of many passions, but two in particular bring the style of this book into focus. Over the years, he has taken up two slightly archaic crafts: he makes mosaics and spends "chunks of time in my Eames chair doing needlepoint." Both art forms create a whole out of many tiny pieces—chips of tile or glass, stitches of many colors. Peter writes in much the same way: his occasionally florid paragraphs glitter with idiosyncratic observations shifting like a kaleidoscope of diverse names, places, activities, and emotions.

Pulling back, however, one sees patterns emerge. From an early age, he became a searcher, and later admitted that "the allure of the unknown and risk of forsaken adventures crowded out the security of good sense." And readers will be so glad he did. After all, good sense would surely have cautioned not just against immersion in the world's oldest civilization, emulation of the Renaissance model of a cultured banker, and taking on impossibly intricate hobbies. It would also have dissuaded him from ever setting out on an adventure as mad as that of a gay man seeking to adopt a Chinese baby in the 1990s. Peter himself describes the latter as akin to his "beginning a courtship—with a chimera."

By the end of this tale, readers will feel that they have read a story about a couple and a family that could only have happened in the twenty-first century yet could only be told by someone with a deep sympathy for the distant past. Peter writes with irresistibly old-fashioned flair. His turbulent inner life is contained in an exterior that is genuinely courtly, a rare adjective for our days. He has wonderful manners, of a kind that cause our own children to sit up a little straighter and answer a little more politely when we visit their house, in which tastefully chosen contemporary Chinese art hangs on cinder block walls. Had he lived centuries ago in the China he studied, Peter would have made a fine Mandarin.

Fortunately, however, he lives in our time. Notwithstanding his own tendency to seek inspiration from ancient cultural traditions rather than the manners of the moment, he has had the good fortune to be a pioneer. He was among the first Western businesspeople in China, a country still off limits to Americans when he was in graduate school. He embraced his identity as a gay man and went to live in London, where he met his husband Julian, the opera-composing son of a madcap single mother in the south of England. Drawing on deep reserves of cultural sensitivity and grim perseverance, Peter successfully navigated the labyrinthine Chinese adoption procedures—twice.

Perhaps Peter's pioneering spirit springs forth most strikingly when he turns from the intricacies of adoption to the joys of parenting, a subject about which both of us (especially Anne-Marie) have also published. At any moment, less than 5 percent of married men in the United States find the courage to assume the role of "lead parent"— the individual primarily responsible for everyday aspects of parenting. Fewer than half go so far as to share these tasks equally with their spouses. Redressing this imbalance is critical if we are to see advancement toward true gender equality. Polls show that many younger Americans aspire to greater marital equality, yet they lack realistic role models on which to model such behavior—especially in the challenging circumstances of a two-career relationship.

Peter and Julian are such role models. Here is a genuine partnership in which both have pursued world-class careers while also stepping forward at various moments—as Peter's involvement in adoption and religious education illustrate—to be the lead parent in vital domains of their daughters' lives. Difficult though this road is, what shines through most as we near the end of this book is the warm glow of personal well-being that such a balanced life can bring.

In a world where families now come in ever-more shapes and sizes, constructed as much as born to fit people's true selves, a family where individuals are happily at home remains a nearly universal human aspiration. Studies show that when older men are asked what they most wish they had done differently in their lives, few mention work and most admit they would like to have been closer to family and friends, a view that more people in our harried modern societies might do well to heed.

May Peter's story of becoming a family inspire many others. In the labyrinths of all our lives, family can help us find a way through.

Andrew Moravcsik and Anne-Marie Slaughter

PROLOGUE

The ox shook.... That is the origin of earthquakes.
—LIHUI YANG AND DEMING AN

THE TERRACE OF OUR APARTMENT BUILDING jutted out right over Barker Road, the penultimate stop on Hong Kong's Peak Tram. When my partner Julian and I would find ourselves suspended on our balcony in the darkness—or cheek by jowl with guests—we were dwarfed by a vista too splendid to be real. It was the perfect vantage point for watching the annual fireworks high above Victoria Harbour. This was to be the very last Chinese New Year extravaganza under British rule before Hong Kong reverted to mainland sovereignty; thus we invited friends, largely from my days in Princeton and Beijing, along with some new acquaintances.

It would soon be time for us to herd our guests out onto the vertiginous perch with champagne flutes in hand to toast 1997, which would be the year of the ox. Since the festivities took place on the fifteenth and final day of Chinese New Year celebrations, well before midnight, the finale was something of a relief; in fact, the hoopla was subdued because we were on the cusp of uncertain political transformation.

Despite the uncertainties awaiting us on the other side of the pyrotechnics, Julian and I were gradually allowing ourselves to imagine the coming of a baby, though we were not sufficiently at ease to share the news with our companions. For Julian, it was incredulity that determined his silence; but my own rigid hush was born of profound superstition. Even the slightest whiff of confidence could be mistaken for hubris, I feared, sabotaging my quest to become a father.

Considering whence I came, my interest in fatherhood was hard to fathom. Having survived a childhood shattered by the knock-on tremors of my parents' divorce in the 1950s, I took myself out of harm's way by avoiding ties that imperfectly bind. Although dutiful to my family, I managed to remain aloof, as well. Dodging a replay of my sad past mattered to me more than the risk of peaceful resignation in the present.

I gradually came to realize, though, that the legacy of my flawed youth could only be addressed by the creation of my very own family. Such forward-looking resolve was no lame effort to turn my back on history but rather to use it as a springboard into promise. Even after accepting my homosexuality, thereby making fatherhood all the more implausible in the world of binary choice, I held to my mission.

China had happily hijacked my life, with Confucius and then the *I Ching* coming to the fore of my intellectual passions. I studied Chinese in Taiwan during the early 1970s—China was still off limits—got a PhD from Princeton, and did a stint at college teaching. Although an academic career seemed my natural port of call, circumstance and choice queered my trajectory, launching me onto the pinball machine of life. I realized that freedom and security could both be on the same side of a coin. How else could I have become a groundbreaking banker in Beijing during the early 1980s?

A few months after those fireworks had well faded from the sky, I received a letter from Caritas, the agency handling the adoption of our child from China. It tersely stated that there would be a lengthy delay in the process due to unforeseen circumstances. The message landed with a thud, denying me the wiggle room of optimism that I could almost always manage to summon. Nonetheless, I called my congenial contact at the agency, breezily referring to the letter as though my charm and cheer could miraculously vaporize it. She was unusually flat, hardly the chirpy problem-solver I had come to rely upon along twists in the road.

Not only was she pessimistic about the present, but she offered no promise about next steps. She then abruptly rang off. I was about to get caught up in the very history I had long studied. My baby was now a pawn in a game being publicly hard fought right under my nose. Of all things, Mrs. Thatcher's visit to Beijing in 1982 came to mind. After Deng Xiaoping had read her the riot act during negotiations to determine Hong Kong's fate, she took a tumble on the steps when leaving the Great Hall of the People. The future was suddenly looking far more precarious than it had on our balcony when toasting in the year of the ox.

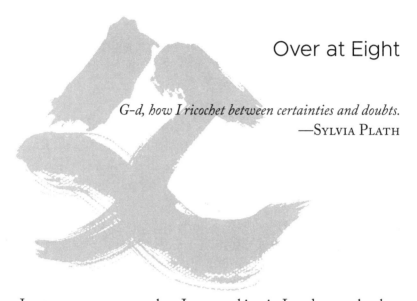

CHAPTER ONE

Over at Eight

G-d, how I ricochet between certainties and doubts.

—Sylvia Plath

IN THE EARLY 1990s, when I was working in London as a banker, a package arrived from my cousin Harvey, who, upon my Uncle Dave's death, had transferred his father's home movies onto discs. While growing up, I had sat amongst my relatives in the living room as his movies threaded through the projector to regale us with images of younger versions of the people next to us. Over time, though, such occasions had grown infrequent, with people able to recognize fewer faces in the films. On a final viewing of my mother's elder sisters' weddings in the 1920s, I could pick out my mother as a little girl but few others—the movies were sadly becoming silent dramas with unrecognizable stars.

The package from Harvey—my favorite aunt's favorite son, who had six toes on each foot—contained a scrawled note explaining that he hoped I would enjoy the enclosed discs of family events. I asked Julian to watch the movies with me, hoping that their charm might lasso him into my family's history.

After realizing that there was little point in continuing to view my aunts' weddings, we pushed on to an unmarked disc featuring me as an infant being taken out of the bath and indecorously powdered. Gales of laughter had invariably accompanied the screening of this film during my childhood, until my mother, realizing that my boyish embarrassment had turned to teenage humiliation, put an end to showing it, much to my relief. But my uncle's comment about it, though wide of the mark, still echoes through time: "Just wait until we show this at your engagement party!"

With Julian still in stitches, I inserted another disc with an illegible label. Suddenly, 1940s Hollywood seemed to ooze from the screen. There were my parents, my mother looking like a cross between Simone Signoret and Lauren Bacall, and my father, lanky and aglow with naughty charm, his baldness taking nothing away from his charisma. Assaulted by emotions, I could associate neither the glamour nor happiness of these images from my parents' 1948 honeymoon in St. Augustine with the mother and father I knew. Not only was theirs a disastrous marriage, but its damaging waves had crashed on well beyond their stormy decade as husband and wife. This stunning couple, adrift in a paradise of lush red hibiscus and sagging verdant vines, was transformed before me from lovers into characters wandering about a foreboding landscape. It was reminiscent of the English movie *Black Narcissus*, with scenes of beauty so intense that they seemed to extort a psychological toll from those living within them. When my family had gathered in the living room for a movie session, these reels had never been shown, since they would have been too painful given their contrast with the harsh reality of later family discord.

When my parents married, both were reinventing themselves. My mother's education had been derailed by the Depression, her father's illness, and the war. Instead of honing her keen intelligence at a university as she had hoped, she assumed responsibility for her father's poultry business, her abilities seeming to grow inversely to her father's—and America's—declining health. Her siblings could offer little support. Two elder sisters were already married with children, and her brothers were otherwise engaged;

Mark, the elder, a prizefighter and playboy, and Jerry, the golden boy, were both called off to war.

By all accounts, my mother had put the business on a firm footing. Then, by becoming a businesswoman over thirty, she seemed to wander afield from the expected path of marriage and family. I never understood how her beauty, evident from old photos and comments by relatives and friends, never translated into great tales of romance. There were cryptic suggestions of her fragility and a broken engagement, which sounded inappropriately pedestrian. I sometimes wondered if the narrative of my mother's career hadn't been a myth spun to mask the life of a flawed and enchanting spinster.

There was a photograph of my father at summer camp as a teenager with a full head of hair suavely pushed back and parted down the center, a lock dangling across his forehead. His rogue eye was discernible, which later kept him out of the army but oddly couldn't diminish an irresistible appeal. There were also photos of him as a jaunty chap astride enormous horses in country scenes, with endless legs suggestive of Tommy Tune's. More the likeness of a cheeky young squire than the Jewish son of a first-generation Hungarian father and Romanian immigrant mother, he had already fixed his persona, one that he wore through life. There is one surviving picture of his parents standing on a dock, my grandfather in a double-breasted Glen Urquhart plaid blazer and my grandmother in crisp trousers with razor-like pleats. As I looked at them, my father's guise came to mind and made sense. He was born when my grandmother was sixteen, followed by two brothers. Ruby, with good looks and enormous blue eyes said to be bottomless, was sadly shot down off the coast of Italy in the war; and Bernard, born with severe cerebral palsy, went on to graduate from college, become an advocate for the disabled, and a writer for the *Village Voice*. One can only imagine the mounting pressures on my firstborn father, which were, no doubt, compounded by the early death of his own father.

I am not sure if my father ever graduated from college, but if he hadn't, that fact would have been inconceivable to all who knew him, his wisdom assumed and sought out. He began his working life at Standard Oil and first married a woman named Belle when they were both very young. I know nothing about their ten-year marriage except how it ended: she fell off of a bicycle in Central Park, hit her head on a rock, and died. That tragedy apparently coincided with my father's topping out at Standard Oil due to limits on Jewish advancement, a dose of reality which, I suspect, took him by surprise. It was at this time that my parents were introduced by Ida, my maternal grandmother's cousin. Years later, whenever my mother and I met up with Ida at family functions, she would burst into tears and beg forgiveness for her poor matchmaking skills—a predictable and heartfelt performance that became something of a family joke.

Each of my parents, empowered by the prospect of a new life with the other, set out on a shared adventure. My mother's elder brother had come home from the war and was now working in the family business. As an optimistic newlywed, she simply handed over the company to him, though it had been left to her by their father in recognition of her laudable efforts. My father, a young widower now with a statuesque blonde on his arm, accepted a job in Miami Beach right at the beginning of the hotel boom that was soon to transform the sleepy resort into one of architectural novelty and unimagined allure. Invited by a cousin to join the management team of the Maxwell Company, a firm outfitting hotels that were to become iconic symbols of the era, he set off from New York with his bride, stopping along the way in St. Augustine for their honeymoon. Had I known my parents only from the images of their sojourn in America's oldest city, they would have been forever shimmering, untouched by the acrimony and sadness that would later dim all of our lives.

The newlyweds' first home was a garden apartment in Miami Beach, their compound painted white with colorful deco trim and planted with palm trees and hibiscus. Their neighbors were other young couples who had also relocated from New York in search of new lives, making for an instant community with enduring chemistry. As they prospered, the couples gradually moved on to Coral Gables, where they re-created their group on a finer scale. In our new neighborhood, the children of my parents' friends became my friends, especially Paul and Terry. On rare occasions, I enjoyed the company of my father. Sometimes he took me to his office, where his secretary named Beulah showed me how to use a typewriter. I could make myself laugh simply by repeating her name over and over under my breath. I also liked it when my father exiled our navy blue 1948 Buick convertible—with electric windows—to the driveway so he could fill our garage with a huge platform on which he placed my electric train set. Though he was very much in command of our new universe, I happily would try to figure out the timing of the trains' whistles as the Lionel cars raced around the tracks over and under bridges, tripping traffic barriers that prevented tiny automobiles from coming into harm's way. Ours was parallel play.

I only remember one occasion when he punished me. Early in the morning I had gone into the kitchen, where a percolator was bubbling with fresh coffee. On the windowsill, there were three large apothecary jars, filled with flour, salt, and sugar. As though under Svengali's spell, I climbed up on the counter near the coffeepot and poured the brew into each jar, riveted by how the brown liquid seeped down through the white powders at different rates and in varying patterns. When my parents walked in, it took me a moment to figure out that they were not interested in the configurations on the inside of the glass jars before I was placed across my father's knee for an insincere spanking—his heart just wasn't in it.

It was my mother who taught me how to ride a bike and ice skate. She also made a point to include me in grown-up rituals. When her coffee was served in restaurants, she would fill up the little glass creamers balanced on the side of the saucer with coffee and milk so I could pretend to be sipping along with everyone else. One day my father presented her with her own car, a green and white Holiday Oldsmobile, in which we went on outings with my friends to the science museum, the Seaquarium, and the beach. I remember her always bringing home a few jugs of seawater, remarking on how good it was for her skin.

On one occasion, Jay, a classmate at Hebrew school, came over to play along with Paul and Terry, while my mother and Clare, Jay's mother, picked calamondin—sour fruit that looks like kumquats—from our tree. As the afternoon wore on, they announced that they were making jam in the kitchen. When my friends and I later went into the house, the chefs, giggling loudly, were having drinks made from orange juice and a clear liquid poured out of a tall bottle—vodka, new to 1950s America. We watched as they merrily shoveled sugar into a bubbling vat on the stove, complaining that there was just no way to get the jam sweet enough. They finally gave up, dumping out their viscous concoction in fits of laughter.

In the summer of 1956, when I was seven, my mother and I went north to spend time with her family in Long Beach. We rented a house on the ocean, across from the Lido Inn, where I attended a day camp. It was fun to play Skee-Ball on the boardwalk with my cousins, where I won my precious stuffed white poodle and named him Marlowe. It was also fun to collect little sea crabs on the beach. I once brought some back home in my pail to play with in the garage, but I absentmindedly left them there overnight and the smell permeated the house, putting an end to that activity. I also recall how I stopped sucking my index finger after my mother confided her concern about it to a visiting cousin who was a dentist; at bedtime, he tied a sock over my hand with a string. It never dawned on me to remove it.

At the very end of that summer, my father visited us briefly. His sudden departure was immediately followed by a fierce hurricane.

I was alarmed by the din of the wind and seeing the roof fly off a nearby building as though the tiles were piano keys; but my mother casually assured me that it was only G-d bowling, and I was never frightened again. When we returned to Florida, though, my world was swiftly transformed into an alien land. My father was no longer at home, and my mother disappeared as well, into her bedroom—now off limits to me—with relatives from up north and local friends tending to her, bustling in and out. My interactions with neighborhood playmates Paul and Terry were suddenly curtailed, as well. Eventually my mother emerged from her darkened quarters but not as the same woman. Her luster was dimmed. And when my father made a rare appearance at home, the tension between the two drove me to hide, unless I was unsuccessfully trying to make them both happy. Now that I was no longer able to delight my parents, the magic of my own being seemed questionable. Yet this didn't stop me from going through contortions to seek the recovery of our lost ordinary life for as long as I was their child— to no avail.

After a few months, my father suddenly moved back home with us, and we spent a long weekend at the Eden Roc Hotel, with its enormous brown crystal chandelier, which I had seen hoisted into place—a memory worthy of a Fellini film. Not long afterward I was told that a new brother or sister was on the way, which delighted me since some of my neighborhood playmates had grown remote.

But one afternoon when I bounded into the house from school, our housekeeper Odessa sat me down with great purpose. After I had finished dunking my chocolate chip cookies into milk, she hugged me and revealed that my mother was in the hospital and would be coming home in a few days—without a brother or sister. Since my mother was going to be fine and I had no reason to believe that a sibling would not be coming at some other time, I simply hurried off on my bike.

As Odessa had promised, my mother soon came home—without a baby; but an explanation about my father's renewed absence was not forthcoming. When friends asked me where my father was, I would make up a fantastic story about his flight in a rocket ship up into space. My mother, overhearing my tale, once suggested that we go inside and talk. With her arm draped around me—well-intended, though complicating my cookie-dunking ritual—she told me that my father would now be living nearby and that all I really needed to know was that my parents truly loved me. Bewildered by this meaningless message, I glommed onto an emotional oxymoron: my parents claimed to love me while also managing to destroy my home and neighborhood.

As my mother rallied after the loss of the baby—a girl, I later discovered—I began suffering from stomachaches each morning. I was chivied along at first, the cramps explained away by my eating too fast, too slowly, too much, or too little. When I let slip that I still didn't know what to tell my inquiring friends about my father's absence, things changed. After having been a fount of medical good sense, my mother turned into a blanket of emotional security, cosseting me in such warmth that my sobs were completely different from tears I had shed when falling off of my bicycle. "My Puppinyoo [her most intimate name for me]," she murmured, "I can only keep telling you how much we love you," falling back on an old wheeze that did more to infuriate than enlighten.

Though becalmed by her hugs, I kept expressing confusion about what was happening around me. Instead of addressing the source of my dread, she went on about love, safety, and admonitions not to worry—hardly words that I could serve up to my curious friends. Finally, after about a week of my daily discomfort, she agreed that I could stay home from school. She tucked me up in bed with the radio and a cup of sweet tea in my favorite Captain Midnight mug. She then told me she had an appointment to take the car to be *simonized*—whatever that meant—but would be back by taxi even before Odessa had arrived. Soon after she left I began vomiting blood and knew there was something too wrong for the tea to cure.

When my mother soon returned and saw the blood, she was terrified. In that very moment, though I didn't yet know it, our relationship changed. She never doubted me again. I also came to believe that she feared an ambush—that I might later hint at her failure to believe me when I was ill. Ironically, though, my mere awareness of her guilt robbed me of the opportunity for a fair fight. Her irate child would always be stifled by awareness of her fragility. I was thrilled by the madcap taxi ride through stoplights to the doctor's office. There were probings followed by whispers between the doctor and my mother. The nurse then asked that I urinate into a pan. Embarrassed by her request, I also warned her that I was not sure I could do as she requested, but I soon produced a stream that only stopped long after the pan had overflowed. With no time even to apologize for the mess I had made, I was then rushed off to the hospital, driving through even more red lights. Later I awoke, unable to move very much, and was told that a useless piece of my tummy had exploded and had been removed. The doctor's remark about acute appendicitis, which I heard as "a cute appendicitis," left me baffled. Then, as I began feeling better in the next few days, I asked if I could try out a wheelchair. Wondering about the whimpers coming from the adjoining room, I awkwardly wheeled myself next door, where a sickening odor assaulted me. My curiosity overcame my disgust, however. I entered the dim room and saw a boy swathed in bandages barely able to move. Almost inaudibly he told me that he had been burned but had few visitors because people didn't like to see him. I replied that *I* would visit him, which pleased him. I was just happy to have a new friend.

One morning my mother arrived with a surprise guest: Aunt Birdie from New York. During my mother's mysterious disappearance into her bedroom when her marriage was faltering, my aunt had flown in to attend to her, radiating a sense of well-being despite the darkness that had engulfed our home. She now did for me what she had done for my mother. I preferred her benign company to my mother's emotional undertow. That my father was absent from my bedside for reasons unknown to me did not prevent him from being a troubling specter, managing to radiate disquiet from afar. I feigned delight when the doctor told me that I would be leaving the hospital, but as my mother momentarily turned away from my bed, I whispered to Aunt Birdie that I did not want to go home.

Soon afterward my parents divorced. We left our home and my father in Florida, bound for New York. As we backed out of our driveway, I looked into the garage and noticed that my trains were gone, the bare platform on which they had been affixed now nothing more than a mysterious obstruction to a car. Only years later did I learn why life in this neighborhood I so loved had become unbearable for my mother—and my activities in it curtailed. My father had had an affair with Terry's mother. And if that weren't enough, Paul's mother had been the whistle-blower, thus ending the ease and innocence of those Miami days. My childhood effectively ended at age eight—only to be resumed when I became a father. The 1957 divorce of my parents proved to be the big bang in my universe. The shrapnel thrown off by my mother's profound disillusionment in the failure of her marriage and my father's mercurial behavior turned me into a diplomat, psychologist, and passive aggressor. I gradually learned to cope with the theatrics swirling around me, but I also figured out that there was more to the way forward than ducking and weaving. I could affect the narrative of my own future.

My father then remarried twice in the 1960s. Betty, his third wife, lived grandly on Sutton Place and made every effort to hover gently as my new stepmother; then, just as she was finding her way into my life, my father bolted, resurfacing six months later back in Florida. His fourth and final marriage brought with it new dramatis personae, challenging the status quo, which was just fine with me. His wife, a well-educated and glamorous socialite who reminded me of the Duchess of Windsor, mattered little. But the fact that she had two children made a big difference—at last I could imagine myself having siblings: Jan and Jack, respectively seven years and five years my junior. I actually took my cue from my father, who, from the outset, acted very much the father of these children. It seemed like we had both been parachuted into a production well underway, obliging us to assume our parts. I resolved that by slotting into this new family I might finally get noticed by my father. How I welcomed the dilution of intensity—felt along with my father's neglect—that had attended my role as his only child! I perversely enjoyed being alongside him in his new role as the parent I had minimally known, understanding that only by his becoming a newly successful father could Jan and Jack become my siblings. Thus, rather than feeling deprived by his pivot toward them I realized it wove me into a family where I could belong. Simply by uttering the words *sister* and *brother* I found myself alive within a new construct—although this intimacy never actually fostered the deepening of my relationship with my father. We each connected with other family members but not with each other. He remained an aloof and volatile figure; his wit and wisdom, valued and apparent to others, were gifts I merely witnessed but never experienced. It is no wonder I would not confide in him the fact of my sexuality, nor would he ever express curiosity about it. Only once did I surmise that he had an inkling about my sexuality, when, visiting me at Princeton, he commented that my vintage Navy trousers, with all those buttons in the front, were "louche." Though we remained detached, the quarter century I spent within his family during this final marriage served to nurture my dream of creating a fresher and better version of myself within a family of my own.

That Florida mansion, though, with its maids and chauffeurs and cooks, was worlds away from my home in New York. My mother erratically received thirty-five dollars a week in child support and held down a job at City Center. I loved my room in our apartment on the Grand Concourse. There were bookshelves everywhere, and I would create little dioramas amongst the volumes, reflecting a current idée fixe that rarely lasted very long—except for my enduring shrine to President Kennedy. I had two beds in my room, one of them always ready for a friend's sleepover. Next to my bed was a radio on the windowsill. My mother encouraged me to hang pictures and posters, assuring me that she had no problem with my changing things around. "Tastes change," she declared, with a wave of her arm. Only when new friends would first come over and comment about my one-off room did I realize it was unusual. Although I pretended to take such compliments in stride, I was quietly chuffed that my retreat could hold its own, even up against a room in a distant mansion. I felt special outside of my room, too. As a student at the Bronx High School of Science, I became a cosmopolite; on my very first day of class, sprung right out of my familiar neighborhood, I was soon in the company of students from the five boroughs. Even gym class was palatable, as though we were being spared the usual dread in recognition of our renown. All I had to do was learn how to climb a rope and touch the ceiling. It wasn't even considered odd that I would be graduating at sixteen. In this rarefied environment, of all places, I could be tall, silly, and serious at the very same time. But as I navigated my way through Bronx Science, my mother, though alive to its blessings, began expressing qualms about my going off to college at such a young age. My father, though, was all for it. In the normal course of simply growing up, I would take the next natural step, enabling me to shed the role of dutiful son. College would finally rescue me.

CHAPTER TWO

Between and Betwixt

What destroys the dream? What destroys it, eh?...Disappointment.
Disappointment. Disappointment.

—Anthony Burgess

Almost immediately after my mother arrived home from work I would lobby for supper, paying little mind to her need to shift gears from City Center to home. That scotch on the rocks which she would have so savored was invariably postponed by my appetite, becoming a weekend treat when needed least. Then my father would often call, interrupting her gentle inquiry about my day and chat about articles in the newspapers that she devoured daily. That inopportune intrusion from Florida, when my father would say without fail, "I'd like a word with your mother," put me in the crosshairs of conflict that had little to do with me. It is no wonder that to this very day I dread the ring of a telephone.

One evening during my senior year, when I answered the phone my father neither made small talk nor asked to speak to my mother; rather, he announced his refusal to pay for my college education and rang off. When I returned to the dining room table, my mother immediately knew that something was wrong. Not only had he fulfilled her dimmest view of him, but his dereliction might have answered her prayers by stranding me at home;

however, I valued her restraint. She neither dined out on my father's appalling behavior nor showed anything but compassion for my gut-wrenching disappointment. Yet she could do no right. I resented her for being caught up in my moment. That I was even aware of her expectations of my father or mindful of her concern for me, though she might be relieved to have me at home, denied me the drama of feeling crestfallen all to myself.

I was forced to attend City College of New York, known as "the poor man's Harvard." The fact that it counted Stanley Kubrick and Jonas Salk as alumni gave me no solace. Instead of taking the subway to high school on 205th Street, I now traveled to 145th Street, walked up Sugar Hill then on to Convent Avenue, a leafy boulevard populated by African American grandees, and on to my classes. To be sure, I was thrilled by Shepard Hall, a splendid example of collegiate gothic architecture—*Love Story* would be filmed there, not at Harvard—and fencing lessons with my friend Larry in Lewisohn Stadium, the legendary venue of summer concerts, where I heard Ella Fitzgerald sing and saw Igor Stravinsky conduct. Also seeing James Brown perform at the Apollo Theater—my friend Neil and I the only white kids in the audience—helped temper the disappointment of my plight. But I never unpacked, even with no way out.

During sophomore year, my paternal grandmother entered the fray. She was forever declaring her love for me, her only grandchild—she called me Doll Face—but her history led me to handle her in an oddly gentle fashion. Twice widowed, she had lost a son in the war, thereby inverting the dynamic of our relationship. Though heartbroken by my parents' divorce—all the more so having been treated royally by my mother—she could not keep from casting her lot with my father. No matter how lovingly our conversations or visits began, her sadness would always seep in. Though she was an attractive and lively woman with a wide circle of friends, a keen card player, and a dreadful cook who shamelessly prepared pork chops, she was, nonetheless, vulnerable, one more maternal figure it was my duty to rescue. Now, for once, Grandma was delivering good news to me. My father was willing to pay for me to go away to school. But, instead of expressing spontaneous gratitude, I fell silent. I just needed to breathe, leaving the messenger in the lurch. Why now? What did he want? I thanked my grandmother in a monotone. Ultimately, though, I did decide to get in touch with him to accept his offer— which was mine. The dreaded telephone was not an option, so I decided to write; but how was I to begin a letter? Unable to bring myself to pen "Dear Dad," I finally opted for the salutation of choice used by draft boards when informing young men of military obligation: "Greetings." After I sent my letter, events moved with swift purpose. I cast about for a school that would take me right away and was admitted to George Washington University in Washington, DC. I then gradually made some room for my father back in my life, the price to be paid for finally putting myself first. But I could never speak to him about the matter, remaining mute for the rest of his life. In fact, the pain survived his death.

CHAPTER THREE

Matters Chinese and of the Heart

Once you make a decision, the universe conspires to make it happen.
—RALPH WALDO EMERSON

IT WAS AS THOUGH I HAD been beamed from an anti-Vietnam War demonstration at the UN to the Pentagon, where tear gas wafted over me and I urinated in protest on the building's walls. Thus, when I began my studies at George Washington University in 1967, it seemed only natural for me to select a course about Asia. Neglecting to read the description in the catalog carefully, I assumed that The Far East in the Modern World would address the moral concerns of this well-intentioned, though ignorant, New York Jewish liberal. However, on the first day of class, sporting a beret and holding forth in a thick German accent, Professor Franz Michael launched into an intriguing lecture about loess, the windblown sediment that gives China's Yellow River its color and helps determine its course. I took immediate delight in suddenly understanding the reason for the river's name and even tried on a lame imitation of his Hochdeutsch pronunciation of the word *loess*. Little did I grasp that this inadvertent encounter would launch me on an unlikely trajectory that would see me not only beyond my family but on to one of my own.

Later in the term, when I first saw my professor write Chinese characters on the blackboard (井冈山, *jing gang shan*, birthplace of the Red Army) a jolt went through me, instantly implanting a lifelong artistic obsession that eventually earned me the sobriquet "calligraphy bore." Although I had been focused on educating myself politically about Vietnam, I had no qualms about a pivot, unaware that a seismic shift was in the offing. Immersing myself academically in China inadvertently provided a parallel life alongside the whirlwind of demonstrations and meetings that came along with my opposition to the Vietnam War and support for the Civil Rights Movement. While participating in marches and sit-ins, and flirting with Students for a Democratic Society—an organization of New Left activists—came as second nature, getting into an actual fistfight was a shock. Coming out of Professor Michael's class one morning, I found myself facing a crowd. To my surprise, my teacher was the object of the students' fury, accused of being a Nazi in the German Foreign Service during the 1930s. That he was fired from the foreign service for having a Jewish father and had taken flight to China mattered little to the mob. I tried to shout the truth but couldn't be heard. I spotted a friend in the thick of it, his clenched hands raised high in the air. As though parting from the self that I knew, I jumped atop the crowd to go after him. With my arms now flailing, I suddenly felt myself being pulled back from the confrontation. Of all things, my friend Kenny, an ROTC candidate, saved me from the peaceniks. Here we were, a violent lefty being rescued by a future soldier coming together to defend Professor Michael's integrity.

Professor Michael's charisma had lured me away not only from the study of Vietnam but from the present as well, turning me right around to face China's past. On one occasion, caught in his gaze, I was firmly told that if I didn't learn about traditional China I would forever be an intellectual fraud; he then commanded, "You go to Fritz." He was referring to Professor F. W. Mote of

Princeton University, his younger colleague from earlier days at the University of Washington, that hub of sinology renowned for transplanting scholars of Asia throughout American universities. Unlike Franz Michael, Fritz Mote had become an intellectual historian whose sweep of interests arced from Chinese cosmology to Ming texts.

When I arrived at Princeton University, first as a visiting scholar following my graduation from George Washington University, Professor Mote was in Granby, Colorado, his mountain aerie, at work on his latest academic tome. Despite his absence, merely bearing his imprimatur eased my way. Upon his return in the new year, he was hardly what I had expected. A slight and pudgy man, he was low to the ground with a boyish gait and puffy eyes that were incapable of hiding the liveliest of spirits. Much to my surprise, this eminent scholar actually taught my Chinese language course, with an attention to tones so fierce that I came to dread the class. But the expanse of his lectures, ranging from the absence of a creation myth in China to the kidnapping of a Ming emperor, was beguiling. As was my wont, I dwelt upon the attractions of cosmology, which pandered to my imagination. At first, I deluded myself into thinking that creativity could take the place of learning to speak good Chinese. It quickly became apparent, though, that in Mr. Mote's eyes—at Princeton, educators of the greatest stature were never called professors—nothing could compensate for my poor linguistic ability. If I were ever to be taken seriously as a sinologist, he pronounced, I would need to go off to Tunghai University in Taiwan—mainland China was still off limits to American students—where Princeton-in-Asia had its China program, offering the language immersion I so desperately needed.

One afternoon, while wandering into a snack bar perched above a reading room in Princeton's Firestone Library, I recognized an advanced graduate student named Jack who had been inordinately kind to me upon my arrival at the university. He waved me over to his table, which he was sharing with a fellow who immediately made it clear that I was intruding. Rather than sitting down, I took my cue from the stranger and excused myself, slighted by my exclusion and discomfited by my timidity.

As though I were being punished, I then began bumping into Jack's brooding table mate around campus. Initially, I tried to either avert my eyes or alter my path to avoid a return engagement with this sharp-elbowed prima donna, but he made every effort to engage me, and I was soon to learn his name was Jim and he was studying Japanese. Though I was not yet consciously aware of my attraction to Jim, I gradually took to him, struck by his attention and disarming kindness. A rapport swiftly developed between us, the depth of which was disproportionate to our brief acquaintanceship. With a thick mane of hair and the ability to drink wine and hold a cigarette like someone in the movies, he would cross rooms to spend time with me. He taught me to sip vermouth while we commiserated about our demanding advisers, the legendary scholars Marius Jansen and Fritz Mote.

When I took Jim home for a weekend in New York and he entered my mother's apartment, it was filled with a pastiche of characters. My mother, whose charm and warmth were irresistible to people over the course of her lifetime, attracted many new friends over the years. On this very first visit, it was as if Jim had wandered into a production of *You Can't Take It With You*, the appeal of our ragtag guests a far cry from his stitched-up household back in Chicago. But almost as soon as our friendship had taken hold in Princeton we both found ourselves bound for Asia.

Thanks to the Princeton-in-Asia organization, I was to first spend the summer in Tokyo teaching English. Knowing Jim would be there too gave me confidence to sign on for the detour en route to Taiwan. When Jim found me at the dicey Shinjuku ryokan where I began my Tokyo stay—its smell of urine and notoriety as a drug den cut the guided tour short—he swept me off to a lovely flat in Yotsuya where we would be living. His very presence enabled me to make the most of that summer. I taught English at a government ministry, took a Classical Chinese class with a bunch of Japanese ladies giggling behind their fans, and, under his purview, visited louche watering holes. We lived on *gyoza* and slept side by side, the whiff of the tatami floor lulling me to sleep as I wound down after proudly recounting to him my day's activities. One evening, as we readied our futon for sleep, I noticed a scar on his chest and asked about it. "It's a stigmata," he replied with a straight face. Even after he had addressed my blank stare of ignorance, stating, "It corresponds to a mark left on Christ at the Crucifixion," I, so completely in his thrall, believed him. That summer's intimacy, born of mere proximity, began a courtship right out of a Victorian novel.

By the time I got to Taipei, my street Japanese was better than my Chinese patois. It was not my poor tones that did me in; it was the shock of hearing the local twang that little resembled the brand of Mandarin—a snappy northern dialect characterized by the sound of an *r* tacked on to the ends of words—that had been served up at Princeton. The taxi ride from the Taichung train station to the university was even more bewildering; the farther one traveled southward, the more the Taiwanese dialect took over. But at least I could write out my destination. I would have been happy to forgo the compliments showered upon me about my calligraphy—I think that's what the driver was saying—just to get to the school faster. I was finally deposited in an overgrown field with a herd of goats about to surround me. I spotted a low-slung building, which turned out to be the "male white house," the dormitory I would be calling home. Gently spilling down a mountainside, this school, supported by the United Board for Christian Higher Education, was as instructive for me about Christianity as it was about Chinese. I met Americans who had been driven out of mainland China in 1949, when Chairman Mao had taken over, forcing Generalissimo Chiang Kai-shek into exile on Taiwan. These missionaries, many selfless people with a true calling, were interested less in teaching the Gospel than living it by seeing to the education of Taiwan's students; but I came to learn of a Christian subculture that proved as much a puzzlement to me as the Chinese culture in which I was immersed.

One evening, over grace at a supper table hosted by American fundamentalist missionaries related to a fellow student, my host offered me forgiveness for having been complicit in the killing of Christ. Although English was being spoken, I had not a clue about what was being said. Of all things, I recalled the affection Jews had for Pope John XXIII. He had forgiven us! It was only now that I knew for what. During the missionary's gesture of redemption, a server set a bowl of soup in front of me with a whole frog listing from side to side as it settled in the broth. It suddenly registered that I had never had a brush with anti-Semitism; and now, so far from the Holocaust survivor's wrinkled arm bearing a tattooed number that I had puzzled over as a child in my neighborhood's grocery store back in New York, did I begin to grasp what it was all about. On another occasion, an English architecture professor named Keith, who was always hoarse, suggested that we go to an event, which he did not explain. Alighting from the bus, we came upon a religious service that seemed disappointingly humdrum until a Chinese Elmer Gantry-like preacher cranked up chants in the local Taiwanese dialect that gave way to an unintelligible roar of glossolalia, creating an alien spectacle that left me stunned. Shell-shocked by their speaking in tongues, I remember nothing of the journey back to the campus, though I now knew why Keith's voice was always raspy.

Despite absorption in my Taiwan adventure, I managed to devise a way to visit Jim, though I didn't yet understand his significance to me. After my stepmother and stepsister visited me at Tunghai University, I tagged along with them to their next destination—Tokyo. Jim was immediately absorbed into our party, and, along with other Princetonian pals studying in Japan, we piled into a room at the Imperial Hotel, stocked with vodka and strawberries, courtesy of my stepmother. On my last night in Japan, with family elsewhere, Jim and I had a simple supper of *gyoza*. As we were leaving the hotel, a woman suddenly scattered rose petals in Jim's path. He struggled to tamp down his embarrassment as we proceeded toward the door. Such public swooning over his astonishing good looks—by a Japanese person!—only heightened the thrill of having him as my friend. I felt oddly ennobled in his shadow.

With my stepmother and stepsister staying on in Japan and my return flight to Taiwan scheduled to depart the next morning, I accepted Jim's offer to take me to the airport. As I boarded the plane, I turned and stared at him, as though a magnet had robbed me of my will to do otherwise. Later that day, back in my room at Tunghai, I recounted that farewell in my diary like a cub reporter not yet nudged aside by the poet who finally understood what was going on.

While in Taiwan I had had a girlfriend, Grace; had been a foreign language instructor; had visited the Pescadores Islands and Burma; had studied classical Chinese—a class conducted in Mandarin; and had begun a formal study of calligraphy, learning to grind my own ink and wield a brush. I had even gotten to meet Walter Kaufmann, the legendary Nietzsche scholar sent my way by a teacher at Princeton. One afternoon I was nearly singed by his intensity while watching him devour a platter of sea slugs he had mistakenly ordered at a casual lunch in a Taichung shack. With these and many other magical experiences under my belt, I returned to Princeton, daring a Mandarin chinwag right off the plane with Mr. Mote, a linguistic workout delighting us both.

As I plunged back into classes, I was radioactive with excitement. Despite my improved Chinese, study abroad had only encouraged my license to write expansive tales predicated upon slim fact. For an intellectual history seminar, I crafted an essay on the concept of shame, hatching a theory based entirely upon the calligraphic components of its character—ear and heart. In another course, I wrote about a compound of words that could mean both natural and spontaneous, weaving a fanciful narrative relating to a Ming calligrapher who used them in his philosophical writings. At last, though, I wrote a paper about Yangzhou—home to an eccentric school of painters and the salt monopoly—that bordered on bookish respectability. Mr. Mote was invariably supportive of my inventiveness, suggesting, however, that I bolster my imagination with scholarship in primary Chinese sources. Ironically, it was Mrs. Tang's Classical Chinese courses, as text-driven as it gets, which beguiled me. Nonetheless, as time went by I drifted further afield, focusing on Mr. Mote's subtle approval of my intellectual flights of fancy rather than on his academic expectations. When I suggested as a topic for my dissertation an intellectual biography of a Ming thinker, he commented that I was free to write fiction on my own time. His X-ray vision of my shortcomings left me nowhere to hide, his challenge becoming a red rag to a bull. But there was more to intellectual life than a research topic handed to me by Mr. Mote about which I cared little—namely, Yunnan's inclusion into China's empire during the Mongol and Ming periods.

My study of Chinese philosophy led me to the *I Ching (Book of Changes)*, originally a divination text, primus inter pares amongst classics in the Chinese canon. The book had a visual component as well, with sixty-four combinations of six lines (hexagrams) parsing out the cosmos of the ancients. That its words, if read literally, were puzzling did not worry me; they struck me as triggers for adventuresome thought rather than forthright text. I was readily drawn to matters beyond my ken, often leading me to write papers on a wide range of subjects, hoping that contorted sentences would be taken for profound thought. Nor did I mind being seen with the *I Ching* casually held under my arm, the pretense of the gesture designed to display intelligence, even to advertise intellectual sex appeal. One afternoon, while sitting in the student center trying to look deep as I perused the book, I finally read its introduction by Carl Gustav Jung. His theory of synchronicity, dwelling upon the simultaneous occurrence of events that appear significantly related without having discernible connections, resonated deeply within me. I had always been struck by quirky matters which seemed to orbit around me, suspecting that tidy bundles of coincidence didn't just happen. But, rather than figuring things out, Jung suggested that it was for me to espy the happenings caught up in the range of dream catchers surrounding me. The notion of chance began receding from my consciousness, and I came to realize that fate was hokum and the way forward strewn with choice amongst myriad experiences. A single strand of time was not the only way to make sense of life's direction. I was being woven into time which surrounded me—an image made all the more vivid when learning that the word *ching* in the book's title meant not only classic but the warp of cloth. It was in the student center over a raspberry yogurt that I became enchanted by a set of ideas that allowed me to begin making sense of my fragmented world. But philosophical insights certainly did not ready me for my sexual quickening.

When Jim and I first returned to Princeton from Asia, I had landed well, drawing a fine suite in the old quad of the Graduate College, facing the statue of Dean West, arch nemesis of Woodrow Wilson. And my spirits had been buoyed by Fritz Mote's challenging support, as though I were being welcomed back as a more highly evolved version of myself. My rooms became a natural port of call for friends, Jim amongst them, with plenty of vermouth for one and all, and late-night dancing in the DeBasement bar, a subterranean watering hole tucked away in a dank corner of the Graduate College.

One day we learned of a singer coming to perform at Alexander Hall—Bette Midler—who had gotten her start at the Continental

Baths in the old Ansonia Hotel, a venue that shockingly catered to a gay clientele. I had heard one of her songs and decided to go to the concert, asking Deborah, a fellow student in the East Asian Studies department, to come along as my date. After we took our seats, I realized that the audience consisted largely of cult fans from New York and Philadelphia. Amidst drag queens and gay devotees, there Deborah and I sat—she far more relaxed than me in my blazer—as I was swept away by the music and drawn to those around me. I was shaken by the anomaly of being both on edge and at ease that evening. Unable to articulate my true feelings in the weeks that followed, I could manage only some cryptic comments about the striking audience that made no sense but apparently alerted friends to the hard-fought battle being waged within me. Yet neither pomposity nor denial kept me from becoming addicted to Bette Midler's album, often falling asleep to her singing. It was also during this period that I bought colored underwear, swam laps to start getting fit, and grew a D. H. Lawrence-like beard. Despite these signal gestures pointing to my emerging sexuality, I was still so benighted that I was puzzled by being treated differently by those around me, as though they were already dealing with the new me still in waiting. Then one evening Jim and I were sitting in my room listening to Bette Midler while sipping Tribuno vermouth. In front of the fireplace, he became my sexual steward, so mercifully crystallizing disparate sensations that I found myself immediately becalmed. When I finally got my bearings and we were leaning back against the sofa—had it been a movie, we would have been smoking—I thought of those rose petals back in Tokyo; but this time Jim was scattering them for me. I finally understood his power; and I felt relief by now being in plain sight and no longer out of focus. The very next day it was just so much fun to quietly share knowing glances as we walked together down Nassau Street—a delight to be out and about.

The fizz was soon gone. Jim began to mysteriously recede. His sudden detachment even prompted me to dash from a lecture that we were both attending; and on one sleepless night, looking at his room from mine, I forensically rewound our time together. Finally, after offering me the cryptic explanation that I had scared him, he left my life. It was long after Bette Midler's album had worn thin that I finally learned of his own gay past. Feelings that had been well hived off and freshly quickened had caused him to bolt, leaving me to make frail peace with his loss. Then, years later, even after being taken unawares by his renewed overtures at the Dorchester Hotel in London—a replay of the fraught past played out rather than the beginning of a joyous coda—the immediacy of our relationship back in Princeton did not fade. That tingling limbo which I had shared with Jim, rather than our sexual denouement, could have survived only within my synchronous world of fickle time.

CHAPTER FOUR

China via Ohio, Vermont, Nietzsche, California, and Manny Hanny

Adventures do occur, but not punctually.

—E. M. FORSTER

DURING MY CHILDHOOD in 1950s Florida, there were only three television channels, and all programs were in black and white. A weekly circus show drew me right up to the screen. I was mesmerized by the female high-wire performers, trying to discern their belly buttons as they navigated the tightrope and flew on the trapeze. Such keen interest in females' navels seemed to bode well for a heterosexual life ahead.

Alongside my early attraction to scantily clad circus performers, I had an aversion to athletics. In Florida, my lack of prowess on the ball field was not obvious because all we usually did was ride bikes, fly kites, and swim. But later in New York City, where I lived after my parents' divorce, I could not mask my athletic shortcomings in the wide-open schoolyard. The awkwardness I felt with boys shooting hoops was mirrored by my lame comportment with girls. Although I always liked girls, I came to agonize about putting my arm around their shoulders at movies, let alone matching the sexual overtures reported later by other boys. Over time I became alienated from the mainstream interests of my peers, but I persevered longer with girls than with sports.

That mysterious power which had drawn me to the television screen in my early years eventually seeped away, and I was marooned in the sexual equivalent of right field, where hopeless baseball players were dispatched. But despite dimming heterosexuality I never wavered in my certainty that I wanted to be, and would become, a father. Even after I had sorted out my sexuality at Princeton, my goal of fatherhood survived the realization of the impossibility of someday playing house with a woman. Along the way, there would be Alice on Grant Avenue, Miriam at Bronx Science, Miss Kirsh in Florida, Grace in Taiwan, Ellen from Princeton, Kathy in New York, Snuffles in London, and Judy from Camp Echo days. But they had now been relegated to the past, displaced by truth. Fatherhood, though, remained undimmed on the horizon, with a career in sinology closer to hand.

With a Princeton doctorate so long in the offing, I had grown restless in the stacks of the Gest Library. When an academic position for a midwestern itinerant lecturer advocating Asian studies based at Oberlin came to my adviser's attention, he suggested I apply, under the proviso that I would complete my thesis. Hand on heart, I bolted for Ohio, an ironic venue after having had a bellyful of keen and earnest Oberlin students during my sojourn in Taiwan. Although I did come to enjoy wandering about Ohio, Michigan, and Indiana, daring to lecture on cosmology safely beyond earshot of Mr. Mote, and giving calligraphy demonstrations—grinding Chinese ink on a black stone with mystical flair before rapt students who nearly levitated in awe—a nexus of factors conspired against a future at Oberlin. It was a humorless and self-aware place, teeming with intelligent students who managed to be prim while using coed showers and who wore flannel shirts in the summer. Even though the town had been a stop on the Underground Railroad and had a fine art museum, its very own Frank Lloyd Wright house, a surfeit of Buxtehude organ recitals at the conservatory, and the most delicious Gibson's doughnuts, I wanted out. Even Cleveland, with its symphony and art museum—and the Cuyahoga River once aflame—did not compensate for the dry town I was calling home. Of all things, the message of a lecture delivered in the chapel by Talcott Parsons, the eminent and incomprehensible sociologist, endures. I felt obliged to attend it since he had been the mentor of Marion Levy, a sociology professor back at Princeton whose glittering wit was left in the dust by his eccentricity. Professor Parsons's message—that religion could be a compelling vehicle for positive change—gave me a subversive thrill during these years of moral disorientation occasioned by the Vietnam War.

But there was more to Oberlin than its town of doughnuts, sociology, and tap-dancing lessons at the college. One Saturday, driven by desperation to explore the nearby Elyria Mall, I became aware of someone following me. Ever doubtful of my drawing power, I led the chap on a merry dance, finally taking a seat in the middle of a crowd being addressed by a fireman, with a glistening hook and ladder parked as a backdrop in the huge space. Without turning around, I knew the fellow had sat down right behind me, the way I had known that Alice—an early teenage crush—was in the synagogue pew directly behind mine during the High Holy Days. I spun around and asked him, "Do you believe in fire prevention?" Thus began our relationship, sparked by my comically cryptic allusion to dousing flames. Though Carter, an accomplished teacher with real flair, made life bearable in the Buckeye State, he could not keep me there. When a one-year sabbatical replacement job became available in Middlebury's history department, I moved there after a summer back at Princeton working on my dissertation, upholding my promise to Mr. Mote to push ahead.

I already had fond feelings for Middlebury, having spent two summers in its Chinese and Japanese language schools; thus, when Nick Clifford, the college's delightful and respected Chinese history professor—himself a Princetonian—put out the narrowly syndicated word about his academic leave, perhaps only to Fritz Mote, the job was readily mine. With familiarity and goodwill already awaiting me in Vermont, I took a flat on the top floor of the college doctor's farmhouse at the steep end of the campus's spine. I even loved its vertiginous outdoor staircase, soon discovering its perilous icy charm as winter set in. When Larry, my high school friend, visited me right after a storm, his precarious climb up those steps, balancing Entenmann cake boxes in his arms, was an accomplishment worthy of Philippe Petit.

The history department had gravitas, and I was intellectually enhanced by its members. Their rigor and generous support, along with the school's noteworthy student body—smart and beautiful—immediately injected a note of sadness into this enviable situation, making the one-year clock of my appointment tick far too loudly far too soon.

Although my students and I were all in our twenties, that I had been at Woodstock and enjoyed mescaline from time to time would have been unfathomable to them. No doubt, though, their incredulity was far greater when they discovered that I could not downhill ski. Many offered lessons, but I was mindful of the optics, considering that I was a young gay faculty member. Well into the term, though, Mark, a funny-looking academic star, proffered lessons, assuring me that he could even cobble together necessary equipment. Then, at the appointed hour, he called for me in the WASPiest of old woodies, filled with borrowed gear. All I had been obliged to supply were long johns.

The comedy of that first skiing adventure at the Snow Bowl was hardly atypical, except for Mark's approach to my maiden descent down the baby slope. I had already felt as though I had done a day's work simply by getting the boots and skis on and navigating the T-bar lift. There we finally stood on a snappy cold morning, the sun blazing without radiating warmth. Then, after suddenly turning away, he spun around, handed me a joint, struck a match, and instructed me to take a drag. I did as I was told, coughing my head off. Pills were easier, I thought. "Off you go," he suggested, as though bidding me a gentle adieu. Launched in a haze straight down the slope, I was swiftly at its base, headed off at the pass by my teacher, who mercifully helped me to stop, though I was not fussed about my inability to do so on my own. The buzz of it all robbed me of appropriate fear. "Now I'll teach you how to ski," Mark merrily declared. As far as I knew, my student cum pusher cum instructor never gave up the ghost in class, ever the honorable student.

Determined not to risk happiness in another one-year teaching assignment—and in the absence of any suitable tenure-track jobs—I wistfully left Vermont and returned to Princeton in the summer. Refreshed by my absence, I was soon back in Gest Library and also precepting in the philosophy department for Walter Kaufmann, our friendship dating from that sea slug feast back in Taiwan. I found myself adopted by the Kaufmanns upon my return from Taiwan years before—the relationship enhanced by Hazel, his pre-Raphaelite wife. Thus it seemed only natural to Walter that he offer me a teaching slot, my lack of expertise in German philosophy of no consequence to him. "Just stay a week ahead of the students," he declaratively counseled while loading me down with books grabbed from shelves in his grand and sunny office at the corner of 1879 Hall.

Even housing fell into place. I had stayed close not only to Alison, the delightfully formidable mistress of the cinder block house where I had lived for a summer as her cat sitter, but also to her sister Janet, that formidable presence—with wig askew—I had encountered upon arrival on Haslet Avenue to take up my duties. Over the course of my feline indenture, Janet had been transformed from overseer into a friend of joyful gravitas; thus, it went without saying that I was simply expected to occupy "the wing," an apartment attached to her husband's splendid library above her garage on Orchard Circle. During my stint that year, there were boyfriends, a girlfriend, progress on my thesis, and a job offer in California at the University of Santa Clara, a stone's throw from San Francisco. I was sent on my way westward after a party thrown by my mother at the Russian Tea Room—"slightly to the left of Carnegie Hall." Larry, my friend who had braved those outdoor steps back in Vermont, offered to help me drive out to California. Had it been left only to me, I would have started out bright and early each morning, fading well before noon and checking into a motel with a pool. But he got us there in a timely fashion, and I took up my position at the University of Santa Clara—a tenure-track job near America's gay mecca. I was immediately welcomed by members of the diverse history department, which included a Hungarian, an Australian pretending to be frightfully English, a gay and gray over-the-top Irish fop, and the grand old man of Mexican studies, along with fine students—a less adventuresome and Catholic version of the Middlebury crowd.

Not long after my arrival in California, the phone rang in my new flat, summoning the usual reflex of anxiety. It was my father, whose booming good cheer threw me off kilter. "Hello, Pedro," he said, using his childhood nickname for me, sounding so familiar that bewilderment displaced my usual disquiet. With newfound bonhomie in his voice, he announced that he would be taking the whole family to China during the winter holiday. Such unexpected news brought a double-edged thrill: the prospect of actually seeing a country I had long been visiting in my head and the delight in knowing that my father was doing something for me. I put the phone down and stared at the receiver in disbelief. Although my superstitious nature prevented my readily sharing the news, it did not take long for word to get out after divulging my plans to a loose-lipped colleague one day at lunch. What ensued was the closest I had ever come to a brush with celebrity. The patina of being a sinologist from Princeton was now instantly burnished as news spread of my winter travels. On one particularly bright morning as I rode my bike to class, I allowed myself to think that the upcoming journey to China would restart the clock with my father.

It did not take long, though, for unforeseen misgivings to sully the promise of my new home in California. In November of 1978, I was alerted to local darkness by news of a distant tragedy—the Jonestown Massacre. Members of a San Francisco-based cult had decamped to Guyana and committed mass suicide under the sway of their twisted leader. Details of the calamity long stayed in the media, which was no surprise considering the enormity of the disaster; the drumbeat of reportage was always in earshot, taking a subtle toll. Still, any sense of proportion that I might have regained was dashed later that month with the murders of Mayor Moscone and Supervisor Milk, the latter a trailblazing gay official. But what really put the boot into the Bay Area for me was an encounter at a salon hosted by Elly Offen, an Austrian dowager, at her home up in Pacific Heights that spring, attended by the great and the good of the liberal establishment. En route there from my suburban garden apartment dressed in an off-white wash and wear suit, I found myself caught up in a traffic jam caused by a demonstration in the Castro, the hub of San Francisco's gay community. Dan White had just been convicted merely of manslaughter and not murder predicated upon the Twinkie Defense, which maintained that his mind had been befuddled by an overdose of sugar, thereby diminishing his capacity.

When I finally entered Mrs. Offen's grand foyer, there were knots of people in animated conversation, indignant over the disgraceful verdict. After getting a drink and sidling up to a random group, I commented that White's innovative defense, though a well-intended liberal creation, had "worked for someone we don't like." My remark barely delivered, a man opposite lunged and tried to hit me. In the moment, my plans were upended; I was not about to live a charade in some bogus nirvana.

With one foot now secretly out of California's door, it was not long before I was off on my adventure to the Middle Kingdom, cheered on by university friends whose good-natured enthusiasm caused me to take pause about my indictment of San Francisco. After arriving in Beijing, a place at once familiar and alien, I inadvertently moved from the periphery of our hesitant group to that of a culturally sensitive advocate, spinning the thinnest of webs to help join societies so long estranged. As it happened, we were in the city of Kaifeng—former capital of the Northern Song dynasty and once the home of China's Jewish community—when Jimmy Carter announced the establishment of Sino-American relations on New Year's Day in 1979. When our bus was surrounded by a cheering crowd waving bulletins announcing the news, our local guide asked me to step outside and say a few words to mark the occasion. As I put a foot out onto the top step of the bus, I was suddenly grabbed under my arms and hoisted atop the bus. There I was in my trench coat, sporting a hat worthy of Indiana Jones, suddenly representing the political progress of America and the hopes of China. After then passing down the aisle of the bus back to my seat, embarrassed by congratulations showered upon me by my fellow tourists, I allowed myself to enjoy the thrill of the occasion. As the bus then pushed on, I fell asleep on my father's shoulder, no doubt spent by the excitement of what had just happened. Awakened with a start, I realized the curious position of my head, suddenly overcome by the alien sweetness of so simple a gesture.

Back at the university, I was asked to speak about my trip. Never mentioning my cameo appearance as a diplomat back in Kaifeng on the top of a bus, I chose to dwell upon images hinting at the survival of traditional culture. Despite nearly a century of assault—the recent spasm of the Cultural Revolution just over—China still managed to cling to tradition. Through photos of proud cooks standing over steaming dishes barely visible behind befogged cracked windows, simple architectural features being restored by people using the meanest of tools, and an assembly line of workers passing cabbages to be dried on the roof of a derelict temple, its steps being swept at the very same time, I was able to impart the revival of life in an imperfect country so dear to me. Then, a firebrand of a Jesuit—I often forgot about the university's connection to the order—rose to attack my materialism, my disregard for human life, and my disdain for the blessings of communism. Stunned by the assault, I burst into tears, prompting the audience to rise as one in my defense, barracking down the cleric whose public assault against me was a step too far, despite his reputation for such antics. On my way home that night, touched by the care of the university community, I found myself again thinking twice about leaving it.

At the end of the academic year, I headed back to Princeton for the summer to push on with my dissertation, ever laboring under my vow to Mr. Mote—and forever disinterested in the topic. But the rhythm of my scholarly grind was dramatically disrupted when my mother became desperately ill with a cardiac ailment. Long-masked damage incurred during her childhood bout of rheumatic fever now came to the fore, presenting limited options for treatment. While my presence on the East Coast was hailed as fortuitous by my family, I not only dreaded the long visits at Roosevelt Hospital but resented again being cast as the selfless child. At least this bout of illness was different. It was easy to talk about heart trouble, a relief from the vagaries of her cyclical depressions which had defied both explanation and remedy as I was growing up. Aside from public stigma associated with psychological maladies, there had always been unspoken dread that my father might use her illness as grounds for a custody battle. Seeing my mother now hooked up to a machine that beeped and measured something was a relief; and her eagerness to hold on to life, revealing an incandescent spirit, made me proud—but duty was a grind. Commuting between Princeton and the city, I felt bearable guilt as my frame of mind brightened when speeding away from the hospital.

She survived heart surgery that came too late in life and a lengthy regimen of rehabilitation. On the day she came home, the apartment was filled with flowers. She sat on the sofa in a dressing gown, its elegance something of an anachronism, and was keen to catch up, as though we were having a reunion rather than simply spending more time together in the course of her prolonged recovery. No doubt the strain of filial piety was showing; but she saw beyond it.

"How's Ellen?" she asked out of the blue, catching me unawares. The night before, we had broken up; Ellen had been enticed away from our flawed romance by a woman. Always taken aback by my mother's acumen, I told her that Ellen and I had gone our separate ways.

"Are you a gay?" she haltingly inquired, her use of the indefinite article, though awkward, alerting me to the care she was taking in raising the subject.

"I really don't know just yet." My dithering reply said more than the answer to her question.

She gradually leaned forward and, as though addressing well-wishers seated amongst the bouquets, said, with a delicate smile and reassuring sweep of her hand, "I'm just fine."

Back at the university one late afternoon, I had accepted an invitation to attend a fundraising event for Princeton-in-Asia, the organization that had sponsored my studies in Taiwan. My brief: to fleece rich old gentlemen in aid of the organization. In the course of one chat with a man who was already kindly disposed, he deftly turned the tables on me, winkling out details of my interest in China. He took delight in my arcane dissertation topic and managed to get me to flesh out my qualms about returning to California. Suddenly applying the brakes, he asked if I'd be interested in working at his bank. Neither missing a beat nor minding my manners, I flatly replied, "No. Banking is vulgar." Even before I could take the measure of my own ill-chosen words, he threw his head back and let fly gales of laughter, stopping finally to deliver a command: "You just get your ass into New York. I want to talk to you about a job." I dared not disagree.

My mind was already racing. Despite my fondness for the university, disillusionment with California persisted. The Jesuits were sure to be sympathetic to my filial piety, occasioned by my mother's illness. Again cast as a dutiful child, I had been given an inadvertent gift by my mother: escape from the West Coast. But it was the admonition offered by the head of personnel during my interview at the bank that branded the moment. The prickly Mrs. Fie warned, "Don't ever expect to use your area of expertise; we want to create a renaissance banker out of you." Here I thought that my sole attraction to the bank had been knowledge of China. Then, while coming out of Manny Hanny's headquarters on Park Avenue, my gait gradually slowed; of all things, the *I Ching* came to mind. I suddenly realized that the old pre-Princeton me, trapped within the severity of a binary world, was clearly in need of a thrashing to remind me of the broad array of choice before me, leaving a mere two alternatives in the dust. Sent on my way with a mixed message, I was reminded that there was no need to remove Confucius to make room for corporate finance. Of all things, this prim old woman who seemed to be forever snapping her purse had not just delivered the bank's view of its own culture but nudged me toward an insight which served me well: the allure of the unknown and risk of forsaken adventures crowded out the security of good sense.

Emboldened by taking the decision to jump the league, I found myself amongst MBAs and business types in the bank's training program, regarded as exotic and valued for what I knew, with superiors far more confident than I ever was about my learning the rest. Although my whiff of otherness did not guarantee success when it came to passing dreaded accounting exams, it clung to me from the very beginning of my new career, forever masking many shortcomings. The faith of others enabled me to push on, with a life-changing opportunity appearing much sooner than expected.

My friend Paul, from Princeton, was already working on the China desk at the bank and had been chosen to deliver a presentation in Chinese to a delegation from the Bank of China—a rare occasion, indeed, during these tentative days of contact between two countries still sniffing the other out. He was to hold forth on letters of credit up in a suite owned by the bank in the Waldorf Towers. The day before the event Paul got cold feet, and I was summoned by a gentleman unknown to me whose grand anteroom, let alone his office, spoke volumes. Standing meekly before him, I was heartily offered the opportunity to take Paul's place and told that my participation in the occasion was tantamount to a patriotic obligation. Presented with scenarios serving up two brands of terror—declining to do it and agreeing to do it—I opted for heroism. The formidable unknown boss got what he wanted and then sent me on my way, telling me that a courier would be bringing an envelope to my apartment that evening containing the speech I would be delivering the next day.

The messenger did not show up until after 10:00 p.m. I tore open the envelope to get to work on familiarizing myself with the technicalities of letters of credit in Chinese, which I barely grasped in English. Then I noticed the characters were in the post-1949 simplified form, unlike the traditional ones I had been taught by teachers who had fled the mainland via Taiwan after Chiang Kai-shek had lost the civil war. Spending the whole night poring over two dictionaries and converting one script to another, I had little time to master the content because I felt obliged to get the pronunciation and tones right—my Achilles heel—in order to be understood by the audience, if not the orator. Come the dawn, I decided to wear my new double-breasted suit, suspenders, and bow tie, regarding the outfit as armor that might protect me during the ensuing battle of the Waldorf.

It was well into the afternoon when I was squired across Park Avenue to the hotel. I entered the grand suite, crowded with Chinese bureaucrats dressed in standard blue outfits, each clutching a plastic travel bag bearing the CAAC logo of China's national airline. An interpreter guided me toward senior members of the delegation. Though knowing precious little about letters of credit, I could happily earn my keep by making small talk, dropping a few *chengyu* (four-character sayings distilled from classical allusions) amongst a crowd of people who readily took pleasure in hearing such retro expressions out of a youthful foreigner's mouth. The interpreter soon disappeared, assuming he was no longer needed, though I could have used his services as I slogged through my presentation on letters of credit, the dreariest of banking instruments suddenly in the vanguard of nascent trade relations between America and China. Sweat started to pour from my brow, so I removed my jacket, which our guests took as a gesture of informal intimacy. As I struggled on, I noticed they began leaning forward in their seats to silently cheer me on.

"It is my hope that Sino-American relations and friendship between our two peoples will follow from our ever-growing reliance on letters of credit," I droned on, according to the script. Then, departing from a flat text that I had barely understood and which interested me even less, I let loose with a quote from the first book of *The Analects of Confucius,* a classic anathema to Maoists but embedded in the very DNA of the Chinese people: "If friends come from afar, how could it not be a delight!" That I had imparted questionable knowledge suddenly mattered little. Sweeping aside the playbook, I was led by my gut in the moment, paying mind neither to Chinese political correctness nor to hidebound banking parlance. The audience met my conclusion with rousing applause, dragging me across the finish line. That my superiors heard only the ovation took my life in a new direction. It was my good fortune to have risked being transformed into a renaissance banker—no sacrifice of matters

Chinese necessary. Mr. McGillicuddy, the ebullient and grand chairman of the bank, offered me the chance to open our office in Beijing.

Posted to China in 1982, I found myself in a country still emerging from the Cultural Revolution, a decade of horror which finally ended in 1976. In a power struggle cloaked as an assault on the evils of the past by Chairman Mao, China had been laid low. Owing to the unimaginable fury of the debacle, recovery was halting, as though the population was looking over its shoulder, wondering if the terror might come roaring back. In the era when I arrived, phones were tapped, mail opened, and my room rifled daily; but I found a way to steer clear of both paranoia and apology. In fact, Mr. Qi, my state-appointed driver who certainly reported on me dutifully, became my closest friend. His naughty sense of mischief was happily matched by my own, and our kindred spirits served us well in coping with the redoubtable Lucy, our office manager who had fled the communist onslaught in 1949. Now able to return to China following Mao's death during the thaw triggered by Deng Xiaoping's policies of reform and openness—known as socialism with Chinese characteristics— she was well served by the administrative expertise she had gained in her career at the US Consulate in Hong Kong. Now worth her weight in gold for her navigational skills through the daunting morass of local bureaucracy, she was not shy about reminding me of her value, styling herself very much the boss. Her presence in Beijing spoke more about the peace China was making with its own past than rapprochement with the West. China always paid more attention to itself. How could it be otherwise considering the civilization's self-regard, forever proudly pointing to the very history it episodically sought to destroy? Such was the political oxymoron greeting me upon my arrival; and its arcane complexity absorbed me right alongside the humdrum of getting through daily life.

The tiny foreign community in residence lived largely in a few hotels in Beijing. The housing shortage, coupled with the priority given to diplomats and airline employees—the privileged category of the latter a puzzlement—conspired against conventional accommodations. With no kitchens available to us, we were a pack on the prowl, to be found at a limited number of restaurants in the northeast quadrant of the city. Befriending the Chinese could be reckless, with lingering fear, not misplaced, that contact with Westerners could bring about political compromise. Inevitably, when overeager foreigners felt duty-bound to stalk locals the gesture came to grief. As for me, the representative of Manufacturers Hanover Trust Company, I was obliged to punch way above my weight, meeting a broad swath of people that could only have happened in China. Zhao Ziyang, the premier, asked me to pass on his request to Ronald Reagan for an explanation about the significance of turkey at a state dinner coinciding with Thanksgiving. Sarah Caldwell, Boston's renowned and enormous opera impresario, presented herself wearing unlaced high-top sneakers to enlist my help in finding a clown for a local production, and Omar Sharif did card tricks for me as he waited to be picked up to play bridge with Deng Xiaoping. I had also watched Elton John swan across the lobby, hijack the piano, and mutter about invasion of his privacy—in a waist-length blond wig.

Calls from Beijing to my mother on West 56th Street were events in themselves; but the breezy lilt of infrequent chats with her attested to the delightful stasis that our relationship had finally reached. It was fun to recount my escapades, expanding her world that had become dramatically straitened by decline. All the more extraordinary was hearing accounts of her conversations with my father, their newfound kinship having arisen from the practicality of my father possessing a telex machine in his office. In almost real time, he had been regularly passing along my tales of daily life in China; and for the very first time I felt that my parents were focusing on me, no longer distracted by each other.

When it was Passover, I booked a call to her. Too ill to spend the holiday with her sister, she mischievously swore me to secrecy about the pasta that she had shared at a Seder-for-two with Annette, her devoted attendant. I suspect that if she had had her druthers the dish would have been *alle vongole*. The chat only grew funnier as she recounted how she and Aunt Marcy had recently attended a cousin's one-woman show on the Upper West Side, saying, "If that evening of Sophie Tucker impersonations didn't kill me…"

But after that conversation my mother and I never spoke again. She died a few days later. Just as I was learning to cope with my new life in China, my emotional landscape had been profoundly altered. I was becalmed, though, by recalling her good-bye when I left New York. Knowing full well that she would likely not see me again, she nonetheless sent me off with a grace and generosity that ensured her afterglow would warm me well.

Not long after getting back to Beijing following her funeral, I met an American banker named David, based in Seoul, who would make periodic visits to Beijing, hoping to create commercial opportunities between South Korea and China. One evening I invited him for a drink up in my room at the Jianguo Hotel—a Holiday Inn knockoff beamed over from Palo Alto by a Chinese real estate magnate. By all standards of the time, I was living in the capital's finest hotel; it was said to be the only building in China with potable water. But, rather than offering him mere liquor, I was able to serve David a can of Tab, the rarest beverage in Beijing. My driver, the masterful Mr. Qi, had cornered the market. David and I had some friends in common but swiftly established our own acquaintanceship. In these days when homosexuality was not yet a forthright matter for ready discussion, we finally got around to revealing ourselves, and he told me of his boyfriend back in Korea. That news sat comfortably alongside the lack of chemistry between us, so a fine friendship came into being. One evening as we sat in my room sipping Tab, David confided that he was in the throes of adopting three Korean siblings. As he recounted the complexity and glory of his undertaking, I could not help but take note of his particular brand of kindness which informed his words about those children. Not only did David first plant the idea of adoption in my head but his stunning empathy informed my way forward long before fatherhood morphed into reality.

It was a relief to be open with David, but I was not isolated in Beijing. A small group of gay foreigners would come together for occasional brunches in Bruce Dunning's flat—he was the first CBS correspondent based in Beijing. I also had a boyfriend from California named Clark, who charmingly wafted about, and I enjoyed dalliances and a regular hookup with an old friend who was happily married. My understanding that assignations with Chinese citizens were absolutely verboten protected me from danger with the authorities. Considering that the establishment of mere acquaintanceships with locals could imperil their well-being, the suggestion of anything more meaningful was out of the question. I quickly discerned that what foreigners did amongst themselves was of no interest to the government. I also came to understand that if homosexuality were not acknowledged it did not signify. Add to that my inexplicable feeling that as a tall foreign rarity with high cheek bones I could simply go about my business, with my wits about me and a sense of abandon. Far from New York, with AIDS yet to be named, recklessness within the rules made for a good time.

My three-year tenure in China was well received within the bank. Captains of industry had passed through, and though I felt there was little I could teach them about their business, China played them like fiddles, often reducing macho executives to simpering novices. They were happy to be completely dependent upon me and left Beijing far too grateful for my good offices. For such appreciation, I was handsomely rewarded. Mr. McGillicuddy, the bank's chairman who had become my mentor, pronounced that I would next be going to London. Blessed by the big boss himself, I went on to take my seat at a desk on the hardscrabble floor of Manufacturers Hanover Limited, the first Yankee merchant bank in London.

CHAPTER FIVE

A Night at the Chinese Opera and Auditioning Mothers in Blighty

If you want to eat well in England, eat three breakfasts."
—W. SOMERSET MAUGHAM

THE EXHILARATION OF SUDDENLY settling into the London of 1985 was only heightened by having arrived there after three years in Beijing. I was dispatched to our London office to make inroads with the Bank of China's local branch. Tucked away behind Mansion House, this outpost had managed to escape closure during the Cultural Revolution despite its cosmopolitan reputation. My bosses were thrilled that the way had been paved for me by Bank of China friends back in Beijing, thereby opening doors on which the Brits had long been unsuccessfully pounding for years. It was not long before I was being feted by reclusive Chinese bankers who gradually suggested that I bring colleagues along with me. My portfolio of responsibilities steadily expanded to include other Asian countries, though I was forever known as the chap who had worked the China miracle. That patina, in fact, long hid my technical shortcomings when it came to the details of banking. Others made excuses for me even before I had a chance.

But certain cultural gaffs were unforgivable. On my very first day at work, I committed the sin of wearing a brown suit—"No brown in town," I was cautioned. Then, when buying a television, I discovered that there was no plug on the wire. After being informed by a haughty clerk that British electronic goods came with none, he waved me off to the ironmonger to get one, but I was too embarrassed to ask what an ironmonger was.

When I would confess that life in London was more baffling than it had been back in Beijing, my colleagues refused to take me seriously, their wonder at this China hand in their midst denying me quarter. Nonetheless, I now found myself in the midst of Mrs. Thatcher's mercenary financial revolution, dubbed the Big Bang. Marked by the disappearance of brollies and bowlers and ripe for technological revolution—along with an attendant surge of creative energy—the City soared in prominence throughout the world. But I was lonely.

I had been unknowingly steered toward Belgravia, an inappropriately posh enclave for foreigners, by a presumptuous real estate agent. Immured in a quaint mews flat with a carpeted loo, right behind the Spanish embassy, I was soon contacted, courtesy of the bank's gay jungle telegraph, by a local colleague unbeknownst to me who suggested that we meet up at the Queen's Head, a legendary pub in Chelsea. Immediately upon arrival, though, he bade me farewell, having dutifully delivered me there in his gentlemanly fashion. Since I did not care for beer, a warm pint was not for me. Awkwardly towering above the clientele in the smoke-filled bar—like a skyscraper looming above the clouds—I soon realized that the cider I had ordered, called scrumpy, was not the apple juice I had expected. Anxiety soon seeped away, freeing me up to take notice of a chap nearby with dirty fingernails and blue eyes of such intensity that they looked fake; I just knew they weren't, since the vanity of tinted lenses seemed at odds with his soiled hands. We struck up a conversation in short order, and immediately upon discovering that he was a painter I let the eyes eclipse the nails. Thus Edward entered my life.

That very evening he invited me to supper a few days hence at his flat. When the time came, I strolled there, passing blue plaques linking the likes of George Eliot and Whistler to Cheyne Walk, which ran along the Thames; thus, even before ringing Edward's doorbell I was already seduced by the atmospherics of his digs, which fronted the river. The charm of it all allowed me to sweep aside the reality of the hovel I then entered. After all, he was a painter. Carving out two spots amidst chaos on a decrepit gate leg table, he served a supper of pheasant and vegetables. I knew little about these birds.

"Should I be on the lookout for shot while eating"? I asked, trying to sound like a keen subscriber to *Country Life*.

"Not to worry," he assured me. "I ran over it on my way back from Somerset last weekend."

Though his mirthful companionship in the short term was a godsend, Edward was responsible for my addled notion of what England was all about. The lateral scion of a great Romantic poet and the son of Eton's vice provost, where Edward had grown up and studied, he had a sense of entitlement which saturated his set—and it was into this crowd that I was parachuted. That I was a new arrival from China bought me some air cover with this privileged coven, the chaps forever asking about someone not in the room, laughing too loud, and always contriving to winkle out as much cash from an opportunity as the least amount of effort would permit. There were weekends in the country, which varied from London only by being green, with much drinking and less louche behavior than one might have hoped for. Tables groaned with chipped crockery and crystal, along with pieces of Victorian silver whose functions were a mystery, the heated plates arranged with mean portions of bland food. Edward once kindly invited me to his home in the Quantocks in the West Country. With its stunning garden and rooms covered in dog hair, I was most taken with his elegant and imposing mother, who, I reckon, was as anxious about meeting me as I her. An early riser, I padded down to the kitchen expecting to fend for myself, but there she was, very much the gracious hostess, managing to make small talk while offering me breakfast. During a lull in her circumspect interview, I finally posed a most anodyne question: "Where were you raised, ma'am?"

"Animals are raised," she flatly riposted, so sudden and swift that the wound she had landed rendered me practically mute for the rest of my stay. I had been summarily demoted; I was now just another vulgar American, being suffered in "England's mountains green." No doubt, had I mentioned my discomfort to her she genuinely would have been baffled by it.

It took me a while to figure out that the English had something to say about everyone, so I began feeling less special but forever on the outside of this crowd of old Etonians. I came to understand, though, that no matter what group in England might have taken me up, I would never have been of it. I learned to accept exclusion, realizing that just about everyone else—including the English—was standing outside of something as well. I had long grown accustomed to being an outsider myself, going so far as to pretend that exclusion was a virtue. Set apart by divorce, clumsiness, homosexuality, and the study of Chinese well before it had become stylish, I had long been looking in, with my nose pressed against the glass. Nonetheless, I began finding my way through myriad English sitting rooms that might very well have confounded a lesser chap. Life was now divvied up between the heady buzz of a merchant bank and Edward's squalid flat, onto which I projected romantic charm, enhanced by his painterly gifts and those blue eyes. Despite my own discomfort "in trade"—though forever the sinologist dreaming of calligraphy—I suspected that Edward's disdain for my world by day, though comfortable with its lucre, might eventually put the kibosh on our relationship.

Before the onset of merger frenzy, which reinvented "Manny Hanny" into Chemical Bank, Chase, and finally J. P. Morgan, a newspaper article caught my attention. It was about a lawyer in Ohio catering to single men wanting to become fathers by arranging surrogates, a process on the cutting edge of biological innovation at the time. I copied down the details; that evening I sheepishly dialed international information to track down the phone number for the midwestern lawyer, not a simple task from abroad in pre-Internet days. But all I could manage was one inquiry per evening, affording me even more time to grow anxious about the next try. Then, after several more and finally armed with the phone number, I screwed up my courage to converse with a man who might be able to make me a father. Back in the bank the next day, where international calls were run-of-the-mill, I decided to play the China card to get some privacy.

"There's just too much going on out here, Paul," I complained to my boss. "I promised Madam Bai that I'd get back to her. Frankly, I'm not in the mood to be surrounded by a bunch of gawking Brits when I'm speaking to her in Chinese."

An all-American Georgetown graduate, Paul always had my back, valuing what I knew and more than happy to fix me up with some geek to compensate for my professional shortcomings. "Get lost and do your stuff," he warmly barked, waving me toward the hall doors. For a nanosecond, I felt a pang of guilt in deceiving the last person in the bank who deserved it; but my quest left honor in the dust.

After timidly asking Anne, the Scottish overseer of the private offices, that I not be disturbed, I went into the visitors' room, sat down at the antique partner's desk, and made the call. The lawyer highlighted in the article was readily available and happily chatted about advances in science and his access to women amenable to carrying the child of a stranger. My imagination took flight, but just as the conversation drew toward conclusion the lawyer suddenly let slip, "By the way, I don't do this for homosexuals."

Thrown into a panic simply by hearing that word—even fearing that Anne might be bionically within earshot down the hall—and overwhelmed by sadness, I summoned the wherewithal to blithely comment that we were good to go and I would be in touch again soon. I had neither qualms about lying nor reason to confess. Aside from fearing public admission of my homosexuality, I could not bear to close the door on any route to fatherhood. Simply reading the article about surrogacy had quickened that nurturing need from which I had been distracted. Gutted by the conversation, I was ill prepared for Paul's keen curiosity about the inroads I was surely making into the Bank of China. Buoyantly assuring him of progress, I then sloped off back to my desk. As swiftly as I had been reminded of a dream, it was receding beyond my grasp.

As I was wrestling with the plain truth delivered by the lawyer, knowing full well that I would be taking things no further, Edward bolted for Australia. Being left by a loved one is a drama for anyone, to be sure. For me, though, it was a circumstance amplified in the echo chamber of my own experiences. The edges of my woebegone childhood had long been blurred, allowing a continuum of melancholy to seep into the present. Folded into this narrative was Jim's leave-taking back at Princeton and now Edward's, a pattern coming to stalk me. It was all I could do to get through my workdays and, come evening, manage to eat some tuna fish salad in front of the telly. Only on the rarest of occasions had I felt this way, like having a diving bell over my head, with the world at remove.

One evening I went back to the Queen's Head not to shop but to disappear. Almost immediately, though, a few acquaintances welcomed me, some asking after Edward, not knowing of his departure, and others about the details of his sailing adventure to Australia. It seemed a losing battle to project myself outside the dome enclosing me. Finally I was able to make my way to the bar and order a glass of wine. I was unsure about how I had just comported myself when questioned about Edward, at once wounded and vain. I took refuge amongst strangers, this time welcoming the anonymity afforded me by feeling awkward. But my preoccupied state did not keep me from becoming aware and then annoyed by a gaggle of fops on my right whose forced laughter seemed to be about nothing, reminiscent of the old Etonians. One of that group, his back to me, was shifting about uneasily, appearing eager to escape. Then suddenly he spun about; barely at rest, he started speaking to me just a bit too soon, leading me to believe that I was providing a getaway rather than a romantic port of call. It was the impersonality of the encounter which allowed me to function socially, making small talk as I realized we were gently drifting away from his objectionable crowd.

Much to my surprise, this sharply featured and sinewy fellow named Julian, who turned out to be an opera composer, asked me what I did, a most unusual inquiry for an Englishman. "I work in a bank" was my reply, ever uncomfortable with calling myself a banker. After all, when I looked in the mirror I still saw myself as a fretting academic, pondering the *I Ching* back at Princeton.

He replied, "I need to have a think about American bankers." I was disarmed because the usual reaction to my vocational confession was either a yawn or the desire to rummage through my wallet.

"Funny, that. My great friend Richard Jones is the director of a new opera, called *A Night at the Chinese Opera*, written by an up-and-coming Scottish lass named Judith Weir. Such problems with the production's dramaturgy, background, accuracy....You name it! Even the Oxbridge toffs couldn't deliver the goods. In desperation, an agent in the mix named Richard Haigh suggested there was some American banker he had met—a transplant from China—who might be able to help. Of all things, the Yank waved his wand, and the problems vanished. I'd like to meet an American banker like that," confided the spirited musician opposite me.

"You just have," I replied, fulfilling his wish a bit sooner than expected. "Richard Haigh is a close friend," I explained, describing the pleasure of sorting out the opera's minor muddle.

Such a collision was not to be ignored. Julian then volunteered that he lived in Kew and had hitched a ride with a flatmate who was a singer, pointing toward a lumpen fellow amongst the group he had fled. I asked if he and his friend—"He's an acquaintance," Julian summarily corrected—would like to come over for a drink or some coffee. We drove to my mews flat in Lowndes Close and made small talk over drinks, his acquaintance eating most of a box of Godiva chocolates I had been given as a gift.

Not long afterward we met up in Cavendish Square. Seated beside him on a bench, I foolishly confided the saga of Edward's departure, instantly regretting the inappropriate intimacy, thinking Julian would be soon gone, as well. I got the feeling, though, that he allowed my words to wash over him rather than taking them in. That he denied me a shoulder to cry on, preferring to wait it out, called a swift halt to my fretful monologue. Only then did he choose to engage.

It was during these early days when we began gingerly spending time together that my boss told me I was urgently needed to take on a one-month assignment in Sydney. A macho dunce Down Under who worked for the bank was about to marry an heiress, and the couple would shortly be going on an extended honeymoon. It was too soon for me to feel torn about leaving Julian, but I did ask if he was interested in housesitting, thereby rescuing him not only from shabby digs but also from the fellow who ate all my chocolates.

After my return from Sydney, Julian never left, and the diving bell lifted; life had swept Edward so swiftly aside that the scenario smacked of bad taste. It had never even dawned on me to track him down in Australia.

I seemed to be working my way through the arts. Julian had no dirty fingernails, but he was a composer, enamored of Russian music—especially Rimsky-Korsakov—and Verdi. Raised by a single mother in Chichester and an only child, he had a background similar to mine. While our common emotional vocabulary afforded us express entrée into rare mutual understanding, markers along the way could easily be misread. As his mother, Lori, chose to present herself, after marrying a Yugoslav émigré who had been tortured during the war—ultimately unable to outlive his demons— she had been drummed out of the north by her provincial family for her perfidy. Her husband had disappeared early from her life and that of their young son, leaving Lori bravely to cobble together a new life in Chichester, estranged from family when needed most. That much of her own chronicle turned out to be spun, ranging from subtraction of a decade from her age to the details of estrangement from her relatives, made for his fragile childhood, rife with falsehoods that left him adrift. Glamorous and worldly, she radiated an ease and sophistication disconnected from her personal circumstances. On the face of it, the sight of mother and son together appeared lovingly edgy, proclaiming her job well done. On my very first trip down to Chichester, I was thrust into a party of actresses, county gentry, an elderly woman who had recently gone to a costume party as Ivan the Terrible, and Alan, Lori's gentlemen caller—a madcap bunch of folks who had been told in advance of my arrival that I was Julian's new landlord. It was a merry and now familiar scene into which I could smoothly slip.

Yet the optics were at odds with reality. Aside from Julian's suspicion that his mother's story was more lore than history, Lori's bubbly cosmopolitanism betrayed a personal discomfort that denied him the acceptance which would otherwise have seemed natural. She projected upon him the provincial expectations from which she herself had fled, ever disapproving of Julian's homosexuality—yet he had two gay godfathers—and always ill at ease with his career in the arts, despite her own friendships amongst the London theater set in her youth. Such contradictions might have been less corrosive had Julian been assured of her love, but hand on heart he could never swear to it. When we would compare war stories of our upbringings, the great divide was the certainty of my mother's love. The effect of his deprivation was an abiding belief that his worth had always been called into question by the one person in his life who could validate it, thereby convincing him that he was not entitled to joy born of value. That would come later.

Julian never left, but Edward—never to return—had bequeathed me his friend, Sarah, known as Snuffles. Though very much a woman at home with the likes of Edward's Etonians, she was an English foodie who regarded herself as a missionary tasked with bringing informal gourmet dining to the home counties. She looked like she might well be at home astride a horse at a fox hunt, but she was no poncy gentlewoman. That her loudly ticking biological clock coincided with my own resurgent preoccupation with fatherhood took friendship on an unexpected detour. No doubt clinging to her as a way of softening the blow of Edward's departure, and relieved that my sexuality was known to her, we were soon imagining a shared life with a child. That Julian had already become an immutable and public figure in my life slotted right into my fantasy. I had read about the Bloomsbury set and reckoned that my own story was tame by comparison, unleashing my imagination at an inappropriate gallop.

At a time when Julian was away in Canada, involved in a music theater program at Banff, I went to my safe deposit box to fetch a diamond ring that had belonged to my paternal grandmother. And at supper one evening I presented it to Snuffles. When later that very evening Julian called for a chat, I casually mentioned that I would be getting married, insensitively oblivious to the fact that such news, so crassly delivered, would shock him. His inscrutable reaction, onto which I chose to project his approval, only served to shore up my pipe dream of fatherhood.

Shortly after Julian's return home to London, Snuffles dropped in one evening while I was out, and the two of them had a drink together. Choosing to ignore the tension of the encounter matter-of-factly described by Julian, I held firm to the playbook, convinced that I could still become a father without denying his role in my life. It was Julian's impassive constancy that ultimately did in the charade, making it apparent to Snuffles—and to me— that his very presence in my life was axiomatic. Snuffles returned to East Anglia incapable of featuring in my *tableau vivant.*

Over time other women from my past presented themselves, enabling my contrivance. Along came Judy, from summer camp days, who reintroduced herself into my life in London. We had both been counselors and spent our days off together. A Stevie Wonder song, including the line "My papa disapproved it and my mama boo-hooed it," had become our musical mantra one summer. At that time, it was not so much my awkward sexuality that precluded romance with her but her glamour. She was a glossy blonde who lived in the suburbs—simply too "fast" and sophisticated for me. But at thirty-five, upon her reentry into my life, she was disarmed upon hearing of my impressions of her as a teenager, gradually coming around to considering membership into my family, including Julian, and bringing a baby into it. I marveled at how wrong I had been about her at Camp Echo. During her visits to London, she grew comfortable in our house in Princes Gate Mews, right behind the Victoria and Albert Museum. My hope again grew that we would all find a way together. There was no trip to the bank to retrieve an engagement ring but rather a carved piece of amber from Liberty's—an iconic emporium known for eclectic treasures—that made Judy happy. Owing to my experience with Snuffles, I paid close attention to Judy's regard for Julian as the gauge by which to assess the future of our endeavor. But ultimately it was Judy's own baggage that did us in. Her family, riddled with drama, prevented her from ever entrusting herself to domestic intimacy. She began pulling away, thereby creating the very scenario she had feared. And then she was gone.

Soon after, bruised by more disappointment, I was sitting in my office when I received a phone call from Ellen, a lateral descendant of Sigmund Freud, who was incandescently bright and divinely chiseled. She had been a student at Oberlin when I was there in my first job in 1975 and then at Princeton as a graduate student in the English department after I had returned from my Middlebury stint to continue work on my dissertation; we quickly became an item. She had been part of the Oberlin lesbian set, and she knew all about me, so, together at Princeton, we both found ourselves exploring terra incognita. At the time, *Portrait of a Marriage* by Nigel Nicolson, chronicling the partnership of his sexually ambivalent parents, had been published, giving us heart that we might be able to carve out a shared life. We liked to dance together, and she made me laugh, her well-honed mind heightening the attraction.

Now, after a decade of silence—she had left me for a woman with surging curls—I was stunned to hear Ellen's voice. She was coming to London soon to visit an aunt and uncle in Hampstead and asked if I would like to get together. I responded positively, filling in some blanks and sensing the tick of her own biological clock. When I told her about Julian, she mentioned that she had recently parted company with a woman, assuring me of the schism's complexity, which came as no surprise. After several phone calls, we agreed that I would go up to North London for supper on the day of her arrival.

Her aunt and uncle were most welcoming but of that particularly European intellectual stripe quite sniffy about my being an American in banking. I defensively stressed my Princeton background and my arcane PhD in East Asian studies. But as soon as Ellen appeared, their opinions mattered little.

The ease with which we fell back into our shared stride unloosed me to face the future with unwarranted certainty. I felt that Ellen and I were Jungian poster children—despite her Freudian lineage—capable of elegantly coping with life, which just might turn simple for us. Even Julian was fitting in well, unfurling his fascination with French literature and film noir with a keen Ellen, whose own literary sense and sojourn in Paris proved appealing to him. I teased them about liking froggie black-and-white movies, delighting in my own ersatz gruff persona, which merrily excluded me from their shared compact.

A few visits later I took Ellen off to see *Eugene Onegin* at Glyndebourne, the venue for the summer opera festival. Having shed her usual tailored look, she appeared in a glamorous Fortuny-like gilt dress topped with a subversive cape. Strolling in the fields amongst cows and holding champagne flutes, we both allowed ourselves to marvel at the splendor and comfort of our situation at this most eccentric of English events.

During the supper break, we suddenly began planning a trip to Venice. Back home late that night, I dutifully recounted to Julian the details of Tchaikovsky's operatic treatment of Pushkin. "Ellen and I are thinking of going to Venice," I flatly continued, choosing to take his reaction, a match for my own lack of affect, as approval of the trip. It must have been overweening arrogance that led me to trust his constancy, never fearing that he might flee my agenda. In fact, the next day Ellen, Julian, and I went to a concert version of *The Golden Cockerel* by Rimsky-Korsakov—an event I chose to imbue with contrived significance.

Shortly before Ellen's return to London for our trip to Venice, Julian called me at the office and said, "Simon came 'round this morning for a visit. I opened the door, and he gasped and told me I'm bright yellow!"

"You have hepatitis. Go right to the doctor," I ordered.

"You know everything," he barked back and hung up.

He did have hepatitis, and I was instructed to report immediately for a test to see if I, too, had it. The doctor told me that the results would not be available immediately. Soon Ellen arrived back in London, and I agonized about going off with her to Venice for the weekend. As Julian seemed keen that we not change our plan—or so I chose to believe—I shopped for provisions, arranged for friends to visit, and involved our housekeeper in

Julian's care during my absence. My parting image of him endures: a yellow face in round glasses, peering over blankets drawn up to his chin; but guilt did not prevent my going.

As it turned out, the main motivation for this Venetian "honeymoon"—the prospect of parenthood—was thwarted by uncertainty about my health. Intimacy was not possible, and I was relieved at being spared the anxiety of having to do a lot more than put my arm around a girl's shoulder in a darkened theater. I feigned regret, assuring Ellen that we could still have a splendid time, that what mattered was being together in Venice. Since she knew the city well, I took particular pleasure in showing her something new. The church of St. Pantalon, with its ridiculous cutout cartoons of biblical scenes covering its massive ceiling, was a mystery to her. And despite Ellen's fierce intellect she took pleasure in my mischievously downmarket cultural tone.

Coinciding with the onset of Julian's illness came a commission for him to write an opera for the Almeida Theatre, a venue of distinction in London. Unable to decline the offer, he had to seize rare moments of strength to work on *A Family Affair*. Over his three-month convalescence, he miraculously was able to rise to the occasion.

When business took me briefly to America from time to time, I happily saw Ellen. And when she came in the opposite direction she was attentive to Julian during his ordeal. With the opera's premiere approaching, she, as well as her aunt and uncle, requested tickets, demonstrating faith in the composer. Julian gladly invited them all to the supper we would be hosting for family and friends in an Italian restaurant prior to the performance.

During my last phone call with Ellen before her arrival for the big event in London, she told me about an extraordinary woman she had met. I asked if we were still getting together in Hampstead on the evening of her arrival as planned. She said she'd be seeing me there, but I knew it was over. Later, at her uncle's house, my worst fear was confirmed as she recounted the profound import of her new relationship, telling me there were already plans to move in with her paramour. The next night she came to supper, cheered Julian at his opera, and was gone.

Immediately after she left, I was overcome by a surge of creativity so intense that it could have been taken for repressed hysteria. Long obsessed with *tesserae* following visits to Venice and Istanbul, I was registered by Julian in mosaic-making classes for my birthday; he had wisely linked artistic expression to my well-being. In short order, our kitchen had become a studio, with shards perilously strewn about the floor. Furthermore, unbeknownst to me, he made local inquiries about the possibility of adoption in England; but being gay was a hurdle too high.

Although now forced to confront childlessness, I finally grasped the import of the six years Julian and I had already spent together. With fatherhood currently beyond the vanishing point, his presence allowed me to carry on, though no one had the power to dispatch my visceral need to become a father. For now, the excitement of having blossomed from China hand to European flaneur, alongside Julian's burgeoning life as a composer, enabled me to take pleasure in life. Over time, though, I came to think I had done too good a job at my career makeover, with frequent travel to the continent through the new channel tunnel turning visits humdrum. I grew melancholy about the Far East, imagining adventures slipping beyond my reach. Then in 1996, after Chemical Bank took over Chase, someone remembered my days back in Beijing during the early 1980s, and I was offered a Hong Kong–based position.

Both Julian and I, primed for an adventure, were happy to pull up our London stakes and make our way to Asia. His mother, despite her acceptance of our relationship, persisted in representing me to her family and friends as her son's landlord. On our last trip to see her in Chichester before departing, Julian impishly explained to the long-disbelieving guests gathered to wish us well, "It's cheaper to move with my landlord to Hong Kong than stay in London." We were soon off to set up house in a flat with a view so spectacular that it looked like a cheap postcard.

I was pleased to learn of many old friends from my Princeton and Beijing days living in Hong Kong at the time. Almost immediately we were asked to a party at a friend Steve's house in Happy Valley, near the racecourse. A great pal from school, Steve had mad eyes, long hair, and a quick mind. He also never wore deodorant, which, we jokingly surmised, accounted for his success with French girls. The invitation had, in fact, come from him and his new French inamorata. Upon entry into their flat, we were immediately struck by the glass door on the loo, causing us to giggle as we wondered if it held some sort of kinky attraction or was a design feature of misguided Hong Kong flair.

After wading through a crush of welcoming friends, I managed to sit down for a bite to eat. Two women approached: Janet, with her magically crooked smile fondly remembered from Beijing days, and Martine, French, heavily pregnant, all in white, and the wife of another China veteran. Janet spoke of her two young daughters adopted in Hangzhou; then Martine told me about adopting a girl from the same place only to discover that she herself was pregnant when she went to pick her up. I was thrilled for them, but I was simultaneously being dared to revisit the prospect of fatherhood along with staring down the cruelty of another fiasco.

"If only I could adopt," I wistfully murmured into space.

"But you can, *mon chèr*," Martine declared, having heard my faint words.

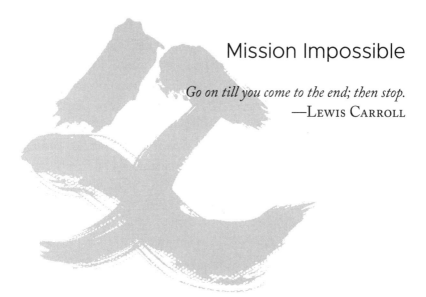

CHAPTER SIX

Mission Impossible

Go on till you come to the end; then stop.
—LEWIS CARROLL

MY DESIRE FOR FATHERHOOD was unleashed yet again, as it had been while I was in London pursuing the surrogacy lawyer in Ohio. Janet and Martine swiftly became my adoption coaches. In my imagination, I was now shifting my sights to become the parent of a Chinese child, which immediately seemed as natural as fathering a biological baby. What could make more sense than a daughter from a country to which I had been devoting my life? I could also now just be friends again with women, not regarding encounters as auditions for motherhood.

As I began to focus with intent on the possibility of adoption in 1996, Janet and Martine offered measured good counsel. It was akin to my beginning a courtship—with a chimera. Preparing for adoption was a matter of not only undertaking sequential tasks, they said, but also requiring determination to stick with a capricious process. I did not realize the drama of the swap—episodes of abiding sadness after failing to father a child with a woman for unwitting circumstances ambushing me as I blundered toward adoption. Equally befogging was the possibility of actual success.

I had never expected doubt to be associated with the granting of my wish; it was one thing to dwell on a vision and quite another to turn it real—as though I had long been praying to a deity to pay attention rather than praying for a favor.

To my surprise, Janet and Martine announced it was time for me to make that call to a Miss Mak for an appointment at the US Consulate rather than contacting the Chinese authorities, as I had expected. Despite my confusion over the drill, I did as I was told. The prospect of simply taking that first step was daunting, with the path ahead strewn with traps that could hobble me. By standing still, I could make no mistakes. I dithered, dodging their encouraging messages, hoping that by merely thinking of contact with a bureaucrat a hopeful sign would guide me forward.

Miss Mak turned out to be courteous and restrained—almost to a fault—on the telephone, faintly suggesting that I show up the next day, her accommodation unleashing momentum within me far beyond her intent. When I presented myself in the morning, she appeared remote behind thick security glass. I could not help but fear that she would remain within sight but forever beyond me, as though in some frustrating dream. However, soon she emerged from her transparent cage and suggested that we sit down together and review a checklist of steps required for adoption. With such matters now being discussed by a government official, I was indeed taking note, but not to her words. It was her authority, rather than the content of her message, that commanded my attention. I struggled to take in her barely audible words, wondering what a woman representing my own government had to do with swooping up a baby in China and placing it in my arms. My disquiet was only compounded by the lowering murkiness attending the handover of Hong Kong back to China.

"You have an appointment to be fingerprinted here two weeks from today at three o'clock," she finally advised. I continued to puzzle over the absence of Chinese authorities from the scenario, though eventually coming to understand that since America would be granting the baby citizenship, American due diligence was first and foremost.

The dynamics of adoption made for a profoundly different ambience at home from the emotional geometry involving a woman, her biological clock, and a boyfriend. Julian had found his feet in Hong Kong, teaching at the university and hosting the dawn classical radio program. I had begun shuttling about Asia as a banker with regional responsibilities, engaged also in the mounting chores assigned to satisfying administrative demands made by varied jurisdictions in the adoption mix. Creating a family was arduous work—much tougher than a quick shag in the back of a Buick.

On the appointed date, I arrived back at the US Consulate a wilted wreck. Hong Kong in July, along with my own anxiety, conspired against a crisp appearance. A wispy Chinese fellow named Jacob ushered me into a frigid room, which cooled me off but did not dry me. We sat on opposite sides of a clinical-looking table covered with fingerprinting paraphernalia. Paper towels were piled high in anticipation of stained fingers.

When Jacob pressed each finger into the pad, the ink oozed far beyond my fingertips. At once haughty and sheepish, he mentioned that I was his very first customer. Despite my blackening hands and my suspicion that things were going awry, I remained amicable as Jacob told me that the results of the security check would come back in about three months. On my arrival at the bank, I kept looking at my soiled hands, taking pride in them as evidence that I was no longer simply thinking about a baby. I was finally doing something about fatherhood, but I immediately feared being overtaken by cockiness. If this was a nonstarter, I needed to fail fast before disappointment could do me in again. Despite my progress, the very fragility of the situation heightened my sensitivity—to others' Chinese babies, to Miss Mak, and to ink under my nails. There was now more to fatherhood than mere imagination. Thus there was more to lose.

While Miss Mak had seemed to think that single-parent adoption by an American was no problem, I had no sense of how the Chinese authorities might regard my particular situation. Although I knew of Upper West Side lesbians raising Chinese daughters, I had never heard of a single adoptive father parenting a Chinese baby. I also kept fretting over the absence of any Chinese involvement in the undertaking. Thus I decided to seek chapter and verse from Chinese authorities about matters on their side of this equation. Rather than reveal my own plans, I decided to pose general questions to determine the viability of adoption by a single male. Since gay marriage was still unlawful and adoption by an unmarried couple of any persuasion impossible, I determined not to engage in public heroics about attempting to create a two-father family. Though China was no longer the downtrodden post–Cultural Revolution place I had known—having been transformed by indoor plumbing, traffic, and grocery stores, with nary a pile of winter cabbages to be seen—it could hardly be a society more tolerant than my own.

To obtain information about the adoption procedure, I tracked down Bebe Chu, the lawyer designated by the People's Republic of China to represent local legal interests during this transitional period before Hong Kong's handover to China in the summer of 1997. I assumed she would be a mainland bumpkin, the image lingering from my own sojourn in Beijing over a decade before. To be sure, it was no longer necessary to disembark from a train at the Hong Kong–mainland border and walk across a bridge and board another with tracks of a different gauge to make my way from one world to another, but I reckoned that China and Hong Kong were still worlds apart. Thus, I was surprised to learn that the lawyer's office was in the newest skyscraper in Central, the very hub of Hong Kong island, and not buried in some warren of darkest Kowloon.

On my way up in the lift, I chuckled to myself about the anticipated mismatch awaiting me—a bowl-coiffed comrade in ill-fitting clothing surrounded by Italian furniture and cold paintings that spoke to no one. Shown into such a conference room, I perched on a chair unsuitable for sitting to await the hick. But in walked a woman right out of a Lane Crawford advertisement—Hong Kong's most elegant department store—in a perfectly fitting black leather suit with strategically festooned diamonds twinkling as if artificially lit. I later discovered that Bebe Chu was also Hong Kong's leading divorce lawyer.

Struggling to appear nonchalant, I made small talk. "Chinese characters peculiar to Cantonese sure are puzzling," I confided, filling her in on my interest in calligraphy, a far cry from the business at hand. "At first, I thought I was simply looking at some characters unfamiliar to me; but when I checked my dictionary and couldn't find them I was stymied. My local colleagues at the bank straightened me out," I added, finally running out of sinological steam.

Much to my surprise, she engaged me in my interest, displaying a generous temperament, at odds with her severe stylishness. Soft-spoken and kindly, she put me at ease, with no rote recitation of a political monologue, the punchline of which might have been a convoluted "no." When I finally got around to hinting at my situation—that I was single and interested in adoption—she responded positively and with warmth. "You just might be the very first single father on my watch to adopt a baby from China," she mused, delivering so reassuring a message that I then dared to ask about next steps. Though vague in her response, she encouraged me to push ahead.

Another box was now checked, but the trajectory of my endeavor grew steeper. I went on to learn that the key to meaningful progress was the preparation of a home study by an American agency, attesting to my fitness for parenthood; however, no one showed me the way forward. In these pre-Internet days, I was obliged to make phone calls at odd hours to adoption agencies back in the States. All seemed to agree that I would have to undertake the study in America, despite my pointing out why this was simply not feasible in my case. Finally, one woman dug down deep and casually mentioned—as though verbally waving a finger in no particular direction—that there just might be some bona fide agencies abroad empowered to approve Americans to adopt overseas, suggesting that I call around Asia for potential referrals. She then trailed off about some service in Frankfurt, as though there was little difference between the Far East and Germany.

I called Miss Mak at the US Consulate for guidance, but although the home study was on her checklist and critical to a successful adoption, the topic commanded little of her attention. Then, after several meandering discussions with embassy personnel throughout Asia, I decided that such administrative vagueness and lack of protocol from afar could only thwart my way forward. In that spirit, I took a chance and approached Caritas, an international social welfare agency with a local presence, having heard of a woman there named Tiffany.

When I tried to call the agency, I became flustered by an operator's greeting in Cantonese, the local southern dialect, which was impenetrable to me. So I hung up. Of all things, I recalled a history lecture back at Princeton. The far-flung empire, up to the beginning of the twentieth century, had been administered by the governing literati, who communicated through their universally understood calligraphy. While the bureaucrats could all read the same script, the words were pronounced differently across the land, with the southern Cantonese twang at one extreme of the linguistic spectrum and Mandarin, a northern dialect, at the other. Sadly, I was now in no position to take brush to mulberry paper, making myself understood in characters that could be read and not heard. After a respite, I tried calling again, and when my Mandarin was greeted by silence I launched into English and was swiftly connected to Tiffany. Despite my relief, I smugly mouthed a Chinese saying that translates as: "I fear neither heaven nor earth, only a Cantonese trying to speak Mandarin." Then I immediately felt ashamed of myself.

Before I knew it, I was bound up a steep and winding road for the Caritas offices on Caine Road in the Mid-Levels, an area between Victoria Peak and Central on Hong Kong Island. I nervously entered, fearing that just one mistake could derail my quest to become a father. I was greeted by a woman who, self-deprecating about her inability to speak Mandarin—she figured out that I had been the fellow on the phone—proceeded to call Tiffany. As I awaited the person who might be responsible for my home study, my mind drifted to old movies about orphanages, featuring fearsome matrons whose role was to deny happiness. Then in bounced Tiffany, an ageless and diminutive woman who looked more like a Chinese cheerleader than a heartless bureaucrat. I had grown accustomed to such Western names, often chosen from unlikely adverts or bestowed by nuns. She whisked me off to a nearby meeting room, where Brenda, her boss, awaited us.

"How did you come to us?" Brenda probed.

"Funny thing is," I babbled, "I found myself calling agencies all over the world until it finally dawned on me that there was one right here under my nose. By the way, is it OK that I'm Jewish?" It had taken me a while even to figure out that Caritas was a Catholic organization. As a New Yorker, I had always turned Irish on St. Patrick's Day and regularly lit candles in St. Patrick's Cathedral, which made me feel good. Thus this gay Jew, hell-bent on becoming the father of a Chinese baby, had no qualms about the good offices of the Church. The women stared at each other, ignored my question, and could not have been more welcoming. They offered me cold water since hot tea would surely hold no appeal to this sweaty Westerner. After requisite small talk, they declaratively offered assurances that their credentials to undertake a home study were in order. Gradually, though, they shifted from adoption experts into gentle inquisitors, keen to hear of the circumstances that had brought me to their offices. As soon as I mentioned Bebe Chu's imprimatur on single male adoption, our exchange became positively lighthearted. Clearly, she was known to them not only as a prominent local lawyer but as a representative of the Beijing government in Hong Kong. Now feeling buoyed by a change in the tone of our encounter, I was further encouraged by their forthcoming discussion of administrative matters; they then passed me a folder with forms to be completed. They also scheduled a tentative interview at my home in about a month, pending receipt of at least one personal reference to be sent directly to Caritas.

In selecting a person to write that first reference for me, I decided not to muck about but to choose the most prominent Catholic I knew: John McGillicuddy, the retired chairman of Manufacturers Hanover Trust Company, friend of cardinals, and the gent who had taken me under his wing after my dispatch to Beijing in 1982. I had no way of knowing if he was *au fait* with my lifestyle, wondering if religious disapproval might now come into the mix. It was one thing to send me to China but quite another to send a baby in my direction. Conducting myself in a most Chinese fashion, I simply put the topic aside. If he objected, he would quietly decline; if he in fact didn't know, there might only be a question about my being single. I wrote flatly of my plan, simply seeking Mr. McGillicuddy's agreement to write on my behalf. I stayed in the office late to ensure confidentiality by not involving my secretary, who would have expected to be doing such computer work during business hours. Being a technological novice, I labored long on this simple task, fearful of inadvertently pushing a button that would broadcast my request throughout the entire bank. Such a thing had been known to happen.

That evening over supper I told Julian about what I had done. Though my steps were still tentative, he, paying a different kind of attention to my words, sensed that the adventure was picking up steam. More than the benign bystander, he wondered aloud about involvement in an endeavor that kept taking him by surprise, saying, "It seems like I was just off dancing in the wee hours at the

London Apprentice…My friend handed me her baby, but I didn't know what to do…I'll still be able to write music…"

He had always been hard to read, but I would invariably hark back to his touching inquiry about adopting a child on my behalf in London, stretching that gesture into outright endorsement of fatherhood. I was forever crafting scenarios to fit my playbook, explaining away Julian's reserve as misplaced qualms born of his natural pessimism.

The very next morning when I arrived at work, there atop the pile of the day's correspondence—my secretary had beat me to it—was a message from Mr. McGillicuddy's assistant saying he would be delighted to write a reference for me. I then approached two lesser Catholics, who also promptly expressed pleasure at my agenda—though Paul, my old boss from London, could not help but say that he thought I must be mad.

With the reference forms swiftly dispatched, I felt as though I had reached a plateau. That I was bound for Beijing on a business trip around this time suited me. I had not been back in several years, so I was keen to catch up with friends and explore the city that I so loved from my history classes and past time there. Despite all the hoopla about the capital's new amenities, I headed back to the Jianguo Hotel, my home from 1982 to 1985.

I decided to get in touch with an old friend, Selig, who shared my Princeton-in-Asia connection and was now living in Beijing. With a brow furrowed beyond his years, he had cultivated a rabbinic persona. But his unending concern about his homosexuality and how to parcel out the news—each person warranting a tailored message—had sadly survived our student days, soon draining the oxygen out of our discussion. Yet his warmth and curiosity reassured me as we sat in the coffee shop chatting about my adoption saga, prompting him to offer insights into the process. It turned out that he worked with a woman who was a close friend of the daughter of a senior official in the Ministry of Civil Affairs, which oversaw adoptions in China. Without missing a beat, he kindly offered to put me in contact with his colleague when the time was right. Immediately fearing that premature interference might derail the plan, I assured him that Caritas had things well in hand and that I would be in touch at the appropriate moment. Selig and I had understood that only by getting the pace right—better tardy than brisk—could an agenda move forward in China.

Upon my return to Hong Kong, I received a message that Tiffany and Brenda would be doing their home study on September 17. In the interim, I was to deliver to them copies of financial records, diplomas, a health report, my birth certificate, and my passport. I also learned that my references had been received in record time, bolstering my confidence. Since I was presenting myself as a single prospective father, Julian could not be present for the Caritas home visit. He assured me that he would be gone before the ladies arrived and would wait for me at the Mandarin Coffee Shop, a legendary gathering spot both posh and pedestrian where we could get the best Bloody Marys along with bowls of piping hot noodles. As we planned his timely exit from the flat when Tiffany and Brenda were scheduled to arrive, I was struck by his generous disappearance from an undertaking in which he was gradually belonging. I sensed that he wasn't simply afraid of things going wrong for me; rather, even if he were nowhere to be seen, he was finding his way into a welcome joint venture. While we both lacked the familial markers that might have provided guidance in creating a family, our take on the mysterious way forward defined us. Whereas I came to regard the prospect of becoming a father as a way to participate in childhood, Julian could only fret, assuming a flawed replay; but when it came to my idée fixe he was willing to consider a life very unlike the stereotypical gay future that he had assumed would be awaiting him.

The appointment was for 11:00 a.m. Under ordinary circumstances, I would arrive early and already be tapping my foot in frustration when the others turned up on time. On this occasion

I left my office at 10:00 for the quick taxi ride home, allowing me the chance to cool off and change my shirt so I could appear composed, taking events in my stride. While pulling up the steep drive to the front door of the building, I noticed a shopworn van parked off to the side, hands waving through the tinted windows, and realized the ladies had come early. I did not acknowledge their presence but instead ducked into the lobby, called upstairs to alert Julian to the change in plans, and prayed that I could make it into the lift before Tiffany and Brenda caught up with me. Then, while opening our front door I heard both the back door slam as Julian made his exit and the lobby buzzer ring. I nonchalantly asked who it was, feigning surprise at hearing my early guests' voices. I let them into the building, leaving our door open as I whizzed about to ensure everything was in order. Seeing Julian's keyboard as I entered his study, in a panic I imagined being asked to play a song when I couldn't even turn on the console. Still, I managed enough composure to greet the people who could, in a flash, either dash or realize my hopes for adoption. Then, just as I dared relax to push ahead with this deal-breaking encounter, my gaze was drawn toward the ceiling, where the fan was mysteriously slowing down, bearing witness to Julian's hasty exit. That the ladies took no notice did little to calm me. I feared there was peril in complacency even when being out of harm's way.

Tiffany and Brenda were thrilled by the stunning view from the balcony of our flat, clucking in Cantonese about distant points of interest before switching back to English and formally suggesting that we proceed with the required tour. As though on automatic pilot, they headed for the kitchen, which in a Chinese home is a place of fragrant magic but, because it is not a public room and is usually a servant's domain, gets short shrift when it comes to design and appointment. Though ours was no exception, being narrow and L-shaped, and seemingly built for maximum inconvenience, they were not put off by it.

Next they headed for Julian's studio with its closed door. I figured that if I opened it wide before they had time to ask me to do so, their interest would be minimal. They gave the room a glance, did the same for the others—not even asking which one would be the baby's—and sauntered back to the sitting room, disappearing into our massive Chesterfield sofa opposite windows offering a vista of distant Kowloon. As they started fumbling for papers, I immediately excused myself to prepare refreshments. Returning with a tray to their puzzled expressions, I mentioned that the Jewish New Year was upon us and I wanted to wish them a sweet year with honey cake. They put down their folders quizzically and looked at each other, suddenly transforming the interview into a sunny exchange. I soon realized that the issues of greatest import to me were of less concern to them than my financial status. Since my tax returns, brokers' reports, and pay slips had all been impeccably presented, there was little official business to transact. Yet despite their ease I remained vigilant, even as they were taking their leave. While I waited at the lift to see them off, Brenda said, "I wish you would adopt *us*." With their van barely out of sight, I just about flew downstairs and out the door to meet Julian for those Bloody Marys.

When I spotted him, he looked like a puppy on alert. "They wanted me to adopt *them*," I blurted out in a childish voice, as I sat down and leaned across the table, allowing us immediately to huddle about the details of the interview.

"But did I leave the fan on? Did I hide the right pictures?" he interrupted, such matters clearly of concern to him. Putting him gently at ease, I went on to replay the morning's events. We must have looked oddly comical, managing to extend ourselves so far across the table without standing up and clutching each other to mull over fine points of the Caritas visit. The waitress had to separate us to put down the drinks and bowls all at the same time. The curtain had just come down on a high-stakes charade that could have not been more genuine.

A call soon came from Tiffany. Aside from being required to write a short autobiography for Caritas, I was informed that the time had come for the agency to prepare an official dossier for the approval of the American government that would eventually be dispatched to Chinese authorities responsible for matching me with a baby. The news brought to mind the old tributary system, in which all countries under the sway of the Middle Kingdom were obliged to occupy an appropriate niche in accordance with status proffered by the Chinese government. It would soon be my time to play a fitting role in a formal process that would cast the fate of a dream. How odd it was to think that Princeton had better prepared me to deal with China than my upbringing had prepared me to deal with America.

As though to illustrate the point, I shortly received a rambling message from the US Consulate advising me that my fingerprints could not be read properly and would have to be taken again. Annoyed that three months had been wasted, I returned there the next morning to be fingerprinted by the same fellow but with less ink being used this time. I did insist, though, that his supervisor check the new fingerprints because I was not about to risk losing another three months over a clerk's lack of expertise. Then, as though on a mission, I walked toward Queens Road, where I knew I could find red ribbon, a color believed by Jews to repel evil spirits and by the Chinese to bring luck. I had wanted to buy an entire spool from a crone crouching in front of her stand who was used to selling ribbon by the piece. That I wanted a whole spool and did not care to bargain left her a tad jittery until the transaction was complete. When she finally realized her good fortune, we shared a laugh. From there I went to a watch shop and asked the proprietor if he had any red watchbands. Although the Chinese can't get enough of this color imparting good tidings, he was surprised at my request, which, I suspect, he regarded as a lapse in taste. He immediately disappeared into the back and then returned bearing a tatty box of random straps, in which he found a single red one. In a flash, my watch was on it. From that day on, I vowed not to change watches until becoming a father. When I asked how much I owed him, he told me it was a gift. He never knew that my gratitude for it went far beyond the strap itself to my view of it as a safeguard against misfortune and a talisman for the fortuitous arrival of a baby.

CHAPTER SEVEN

Might It Be Inigo?

Heaven is about to stir,
Do not chatter so.
—Mencius, quoting *The Book of Odes* (254)

As 1996 BEGAN WINDING DOWN, the red charms seemed to be working. Tiffany called to let me know that my home study had been approved and I was now authorized to file my adoption application at the US Consulate, bringing my submission closer to Chinese consideration. Julian and I saw the year out with friends on our balcony, gaping at a glorious display of fireworks, the last on the watch of the English. With 1997 would come the handover of Hong Kong to China and hopefully the handover of a baby to me; but the ensuing political drama that ensnared us personally only served to again summon my regard for the wisdom of inadvertent circumstances.

At the beginning of 1997, I allowed myself to make a prospective baby seem real by officially considering a name. Despite the complexities of my relationship with my mother, I had long hoped to call the baby Harriet—and in Hebrew, Yita—giving my mother another chance at life through a granddaughter and the baby, whom I'd hoped to nickname Hattie, the power to bestow miracles. Then there was Marcella, a middle name after my Aunt

Marcy. The elder sister of my mother, hers was a visceral force that lovingly saw me through the dramas of my childhood, ironing out her sister's periodic episodes of instability. All I had to do was retrieve aromas from her kitchen—so readily available from a handy drawer in my memory bank—to again be embraced by the warmest sense of well-being imaginable. Aunt Marcy engendered constancy and peace during sad times, but she would also graciously recede to make room for my emotionally resurrected mother, radiant and sage anew, again able to impart her spontaneous brand of wisdom, always with a genial twist. The choice of names did not bother Julian. Although his late father, Emil, qualified to be remembered in keeping with the Ashkenazi custom of honoring the dead, his absence from Julian's life did not render the inclusion of his name a natural thing; but I would have readily made room for him as a way of enriching the narrative of our newly created family.

Julian's innate sense of caution had displaced his indifference to the coming of a child. One sleepy Saturday he commented that I had no real grasp of the changes that would be coming, with such relaxing weekends a likely casualty of parenthood. Rather than lamenting an end to the pleasures of listening to the World Service on the radio as I stared out the window without focus, I chose to demonstrate that it would be no sacrifice for this exuberant prospective father to give up such things. Sounding like a social director, I suddenly urged that we go off to the Jade Market, the Bird Market, Shanghai Tang for new bathrobes, and finally to the framer to pick up a subversive painting of a dog—in the form and colors of the Vietnam flag—we had bought on a trip to Southeast Asia. We did it all, and by the time we got home in late afternoon, though furtively knackered, I feigned friskiness, determined to show Julian just how hardy I was. There was little time for a lie-down anyway—since we were shortly due out in Stanley for supper with friends. "Dog mess," as we amusingly referred to Julian's delicious noodle or rice concoctions, in front of the telly would have been much more to my liking that evening.

A surprise party in a private room at Lucy's Restaurant in Stanley awaited me to celebrate my forty-ninth birthday. The event seemed naturally to give way to freewheeling chitchat about the coming of a baby. Ruth, a brilliant and comical friend who had a young daughter, flatly commented that both of us were lucky not to be nursing. Then she turned to buxom Martine, my adoption mentor, and quipped, "Speaking of torpedoes, are you still breastfeeding?" But it was someone I did not know well, Christine, seated across the table from me, who would grow in significance as the adoption approached.

Christine, a legendary headhunter in the Far East, had been married to a chap I met when joining Manufacturers Hanover Trust Company in 1979. My entry into banking had been bumpy, and his courtesies had helped me through a rite of professional passage that was alien to a Ming dynasty historian. That he turned out to be gay and later abandoned Christine in Japan were pieces of a puzzle yet unknown to me. At the party that night, Christine spoke of "Operation Hattie," baby furniture, and a nanny whom she highly recommended. Her breezy banter made my superstitious reserve seem like nonsense, and her optimism went a long way to transform Hattie the hologram into Hattie my child.

Along with talk of Hattie, the conversation inevitably veered to the return of Hong Kong to China. It was 1997, and there stood Emily Lau, a heroic pro-democracy advocate, right alongside Tung Chee-hwa, the chief executive-designate, who defied logic by proclaiming that "the repeal of civil liberty laws would help the community." Later in January, Queen Elizabeth's silhouette would disappear from local postage stamps, and it became known that local Chinese who wanted British passports would not be able to get them, but the indigenous Indian population, who didn't want passports, could get them. I thought back to Margaret Thatcher's visit to Beijing in 1982, when she had anointed the negotiations and then stumbled on the steps as she made her way out of the

Great Hall of the People. Without knowing any of the details about what had transpired behind closed doors, my Chinese friends had pronounced the deal done, dismissing "one country, two systems" as little more than a slogan providing air cover for the retreating British. That was now all happening.

Neither anxiety about parenthood nor the future of Hong Kong could prevent our getting swept up in Chinese New Year's festivities. Julian and I were overwhelmed by obligations to attend banquets and even assailed by the clacking of mahjong tiles as we strolled through winding alleys. The crowds at the Victoria Park flower market increased daily as the holiday approached, with enthusiasm linked to the size of the forced blossoms. People tried to purchase flowers that were just right—neither too early, when they were buds and the prices were high, nor too late, when the flowers were past their prime and the bargains not worthwhile.

Upon arriving at the mobbed park, we seemed to have come upon a Chinese version of the Hajj, with no one going in the same direction as people ambled about the flower stalls, rarely committing to swift purchases. It was hard to believe that the fierce Cantonese exchanges between florists and customers were about the pace of opening petals. I could only marvel at such a rambunctious crowd being so attuned to the intricacies of horticulture. Then I spotted those strange yellow protuberances that look like blown-up surgical gloves on stalks and recalled my first Chinese New Year in Hong Kong a quarter of a century earlier, when I had set eyes on *huangguizi* (yellow precious things), also called *wu dai tong tang* (five generations one house). The joy of seeing them again prompted a gleeful explanation to Julian, who joined in gathering up armfuls of the oddities, to the delight of onlookers who could not fathom our excitement. When we finally located a taxi, the driver remotely opened the door with a bored smirk as we twisted into the back seat like contortionists, with the stalks awkwardly piled in random directions. Once home, I headed straight for my grandmother's huge Chinese cloisonné vase that I'd long been dragging around the world. As Julian began filling it with the exotic flora, I burst out laughing, owing to his inevitably lopsided sense of design. He immediately cited his default explanation for such cockeyed moments: his mother had changed him from being a lefty to a righty, a defense making perfect sense only to him.

But the artistry mattered little. The combination seemed to blend my own tradition with that of the arrival of a Chinese baby. The coming together of the vase, the blooms, and a child struck me as significant, though I was unable to articulate just why. Nonetheless, I was forever hoping that a mounting tally of symbols would rev up positive momentum and propel us toward fatherhood. Julian was just relieved that I had not second-guessed his flair.

With the vase placed just so in our sitting room, I listened to a message from Bebe Chu on the answering machine, asking me to pay her a visit the following morning. My anxiety level immediately soared since little usually goes on during the days leading up to Chinese New Year. I stared at the vase, suddenly struggling to take heart in the hopeful image I had just contrived.

The next day, Bebe Chu strode into the conference room resplendent in a crisp red suit befitting the holiday. That she made small talk about family festivities diminished the sense of urgency. I even took comfort in her outfit, deluding myself into thinking that if the news were bad she certainly wouldn't be dressed so vibrantly. I was so busy enhancing frail signs of optimism that her initial words about a baby were lost on me.

"The Chinese government would consider a son for you," she said more than once, knowing I had not taken in the offer immediately. My ensuing shock was well-founded. It was precisely because of China's one-child policy that I was able to pursue adoption. The country was awash in baby girls because of the premium placed on sons; thus, to be offered a boy indicated that my application was being given special consideration. Had it been decided that a son would be better suited to a single father, I wondered? Seconds of silence allowed me to consider how difficult it might be for a little boy to have two fathers awkwardly cheering him on at sporting events—a scenario I found difficult even to imagine. I chose to appear indifferent to her suggestion, expressing certainty that the right child would find me. Once out of her office, it dawned on me that Harriet might turn out to be Inigo, Anglo-Saxon for Ignatius, a name I had long loved ever since hearing of Inigo Jones, Shakespeare's contemporary and distinguished architect. I wandered around Central in a daze. Not only was my child becoming real but so was the possibility of a boy. While Julian and I had never considered a son—quite frankly, we preferred a daughter—that one might be on offer pleased me only insofar as calling attention to the fact that my file was actually being read in some faraway Chinese office. I started to feel delightfully ordinary: like any other expectant parent, I did not know the sex of my child.

Intimations of a baby were coming thick and fast. Soon I had to return to Bebe Chu's office to sign documents; Tiffany asked for yet another set of tax returns; and our new friend Christine said she wanted us to meet a nanny named Luna, a Filipina who was a dear friend of her own two helpers. Alongside this personal agenda, pedestrian life continued: preparation for the Asian Development Bank meeting in Bangkok, step aerobics class, late-night calligraphy in preparation for my show at the American Club, and Julian's work on a new piece called *The Uninvited*—unrelated to the coming of a baby. On St. Valentine's Day, happily at home, Julian prepared ostrich "dog mess," which we enjoyed in bed in front of the telly. Unable to find either something deep and noir for Julian or broad and shallow for me, we ended up watching *Savoir Faire— Make Every Day Entertaining*, a show presided over by an earnest Canadian who shared decorating tips. The episode focused on dining room tables cluttered with gilded pinecones and motley ribbons. Howling with laughter, we realized that nothing could have been further from our sensibilities, as our floors were strewn with carpets, walls covered in art, and surfaces cluttered with exotica from world travels. There would be no way to baby-proof this house.

CHAPTER EIGHT

Shifting Gears

When you change the way you look at things,
the things you look at change.

—Max Planck

On May 3, rogue news threatened our plans. A letter arrived from Caritas informing me of a multi-month delay in the adoption procedure, offering no explanation. I called Tiffany in a panic to discuss the terse message.

She seemed to be expecting my call. "Your file has not been singled out," she flatly reported, her usual lilt absent from the comment that was anything but comforting. "Beijing is swamped. There is nothing to be done," she continued, sounding as though she wanted out of the conversation.

There was no need to replay her comments. My pigheaded optimism had failed me immediately. Feeling both crestfallen and punished—had I turned a blind eye to superstition?—I fell back into our sofa, laid low by uncertainty and drifting again toward defeat. My eyes wandered aimlessly beyond our windows, with no vanishing point in sight. Then the memory of Tiffany and Brenda's visit to this room trickled into my blank mind, gradually making way for a glimmer of resolve, dispelling the blur before me. True to form, when faced with this existential quandary—an indefinite delay of the adoption—I became a tactician and immediately phoned Selig in Beijing. Remembering that a woman in his office was well-connected in the ministry overseeing adoptions, I asked him to confirm my recollection and provide a few details. Though I thought I had shown great restraint in my delivery, he clearly sensed my anxiety. After minimal small talk, he told me about Yifei, his colleague who might be able to help. Then came one of those moments of agony: what do I now do with this information? Drawing a blank, I needed to do something remote from my predicament, suspending thought in order to plow through it. Of all things, a Thanksgiving back in London came to mind. When I discovered that the turkey wouldn't fit into the oven, I walked out of the kitchen to the tape player and started dancing to David Bowie singing "Young Americans."

In a mood of kindred vexation, I now readied myself to do some calligraphy. With paper laid out and held in place by weights, brushes balanced on a rest, and ink finely ground, I let fly with sudden bursts of energy, cranking out several versions of the character for ox, the animal representing the year 1997 in the Chinese zodiac. With my energy spent—there are only four strokes in the character!—and a few beads of sweat on my brow, I sat down and emotionally regrouped. Having already been privy to my stress-induced routines in the past, Julian knew he had to wade in. We discussed the situation, and an immediate way forward materialized. I called Tiffany back, suggesting that friends in Beijing might be in a position to assist in circumventing the roadblock. She asked me who my ultimate contact was; I called Selig back and got the name of a Mr. Xu, a bureaucrat who was to become critical to the adoption of my daughter and a hovering figure in my family's evolving future. Tiffany confirmed that Mr. Xu was indeed a prominent official, well-known to her colleague in Beijing. However, when I then asked who her colleague was up north, Tiffany would not divulge a name, quickly freeing me to explore irregular routes to fatherhood. For fear of acting recklessly, though, I vowed to do nothing to jeopardize our relationship, mindful of the role that Caritas might still play in the adoption.

I finally allowed myself to confide in Selig during a subsequent conversation. He suggested that when I was next in Beijing he would arrange for me to meet Yifei. As it happened, a business trip had already been scheduled. After I told him of my plans, Selig requested that I bring two boxed ties along with me—one Hermès, one Dunhill. The ballet was beginning, but, rather than seeing these costly tokens as bribes, I preferred to regard them as markers along the way of a shared endeavor. They secured a relationship, obliging the recipient to take the next step. Gift giving does not survive a failed alliance, only a thriving one.

In short order, I was up in Beijing and meeting Yifei in her office. Poised, formal, and armed with an American MBA—part of that early wave of Chinese students allowed to study abroad— Yifei was hard to read. Determined to speak English peppered with clumsy English slang, she pretended to ignore the posh shopping bag at my side. I let the charade play out, finally placing the bag on her desk and suggesting that she not simply pass it along to unknown recipients without first checking its contents. A third package inside was meant for her. Selig had mentioned that she was fond of perfume so I had brought her a bottle of Joy, a scent I knew not only by reputation but by recollection since it was my mother's favorite. Yifei acknowledged nothing—by custom, not rudeness—nor did she later write me a thank-you note. Since the perfume had been left unwrapped, swathed only in colorful tissue paper, she did catch sight of the brand and let slip that a mutual friend named Geoff, who had approached her for similar help, had only managed a bottle of cheap toilet water. I then left her with sections of the adoption file that would assist her in identifying my case. She casually mentioned that Mr. Xu, the senior official in my ultimate sights, was out of town on urgent business. I calmly assured her of my patient trust, revealing neither my anxiety nor my determination. This meeting began the delicate crafting of a web of relationships that would prove critical to the success of the adoption.

After the meeting, I was so stressed that I allowed myself to be convinced into going to Friday night services with Selig at a makeshift synagogue in the newly developed Kunlun tower block. The service turned out to be a comical diversion, during which an imported Reform rabbi from Hong Kong made us do breathing exercises to happy-clappy guitar music, an activity so ridiculous that the day's dramas dissolved as my giggling got out of hand.

The next day I had arranged to meet Madam Bai, my Bank of China overseer and bête noire during my early stint in Beijing, now an international banker of stature. When I had first arrived in China years before, she had looked every inch the Maoist in a baggy blue unisex cotton suit, black cloth shoes now considered chic by ladies who do Pilates, National Health glasses, and a scowl—framed by a severe and artless haircut—that insinuated I could do nothing right. She became a friend when we had later both been posted to London. At our first meeting there, I had been stunned by her transformation in the fresh air of the West; and at our lunch this day in Beijing's Grand Hotel she was very much the cosmopolitan executive. She immediately recalled what I had pointed out in London long ago—that in England she, too, far away from home, had become an outsider. She had taken away from that encounter an inkling of how I must have felt during those puzzling days back in 1980s Beijing. Now, over crystal, too much cutlery, and napkins brittle with starch, she commented on how those words had affected her own relations with foreigners when she returned to Beijing. During our wistful reminiscence about the dumplings and *pu ding* (the Chinese version of flan) in the Stalinist restaurant of the hotel's old wing, I introduced my adoption plans, and she kindly asked how she could help. Considering that her role had once been that of a fearsome apparatchik, I was touched by her willingness to assist me in becoming a father.

Immediately upon my arrival back in Hong Kong, I wanted to find out what I could send Yifei as both an expression of my gratitude for her help as well as a passive-aggressive prod to maintain her attention. Word came back from Selig that she liked Hermès scarves. I had once been in a Hermès store in London and, both intimidated and bemused by the place, vowed never to return. But there I was, entering the Hong Kong store and, after nervously looking through a wide selection of scarves, drawn to a blue one with flowers, its color right from a Ming vase. Maintaining adoption momentum was paramount to me, so I pondered how I could get the scarf to Beijing in a timely fashion. Mailing it was out of the question since it would surely be pinched, ending up around a postal worker's neck. I suddenly recalled that Selig would be joining us on an upcoming holiday to Mongolia with a group of Princetonians and that I could ask him to take the scarf back to Yifei. Soon I was packing grubby clothes for a grasslands adventure, topping off my rucksack with a Hermès bag.

The scarf successfully reached Yifei via Mongolia, courtesy of Selig, and she subsequently called me in Hong Kong to say she had discussed the matter with Mr. Xu, who recounted a litany of problems obstructing my way and finally asked, "Why should I help?" Though mindful of Yifei's relationship with Mr. Xu, I nonetheless felt that the scarf had given me certain rights, and I asked if a deal was being suggested. She said, with some discomfort, "Yes." After some debate, we settled on an amount of $3,000, which could have been a fee, a bribe, or a hybrid payment. Yifei then mentioned her close friendship with Iris, Mr. Xu's daughter and a classmate in her MBA program, adding that Iris was thinking of getting into adoption services. I then shifted attention from father to daughter, suggesting seed money for Iris the entrepreneur rather than her father the government official. Although Yifei kept saying I should speak directly to Mr. Xu or Iris, the prospect terrified me, and I declined. My own discomfort must have been palpable, so she consented to persevere on my behalf.

Yifei's next call was both vague and disturbing. Evidently, there was now a problem with Caritas's certification to act as an adoption agency in China—fleshing out the pause reported by Tiffany—and my file could not be located. Furthermore, Iris was amenable to a "business" discussion; the time for direct communication had come, Yifei declared. When I asked her for guidance, she made only two suggestions: let Iris come up with her own financial proposition and do not impart knowledge of her father's prominence in the government. I had come to trust Yifei when it came to such matters, getting me beyond the need for logic. It was time for me to play my part in a masque where the actors understood their roles, if not the play. All that mattered was the finale.

I agonized over the phone call to Iris but finally made it. Although Yifei had clearly prepped her for the conversation—Iris was clear about my quarry—her tone remained general. She, too, finally asked me to send along key documents that could help identify my file. She told me that she would be in touch when she arrived in Hong Kong, where she and her Cantonese husband would soon be setting up a household, though her four-month-old child would be staying behind up north.

As promised, Iris contacted me when she got to Hong Kong. The news was not good. Her father had withdrawn Caritas's authority to pursue adoptions on the mainland. Now I understood the severe extent of Tiffany's cryptic letter informing me of the delay. The agency and my case had been casualties of the handover of Hong Kong to China, painful signals marking the territory's return to the motherland. Beijing's political muscle was to be deeply felt well beyond rhetoric, ranging from a new military presence to denying me my baby. Furthermore, there were bilateral problems between America and China. "Do you realize that there are one hundred and twenty agencies all over the States in the adoption business?" she snapped, sounding as though she might be mimicking her father, the authoritative official. It was hard to discern, as well, if she had actually located my file. I offered to fax her relevant materials, along with other bits and pieces—to beef up the file—and keep communication alive. Iris agreed, giving me her Hong Kong details. Running purely on adrenaline, I sent off the papers and scrawled a hasty postscript in Chinese, inviting her to lunch in the next few days.

The taxi ride home was a depressing one, heightened by Julian's absence from the scene. While his new opera, *The Uninvited*, was triumphing in London—the very first of his I had missed—I was having to confront the prospect of failure yet again. Then, as I was entering my front door, the phone rang. Iris was calling to say lunch would be fine, commenting that she had been taken aback by my calligraphy of traditional characters rather than the simplified versions. Since my Chinese education had begun in America and Taiwan, where my émigré teachers had turned their backs on the mainland, I had only been taught the traditional versions of characters; my script had not been an artistic choice.

On the morning of our lunch appointment, I called to suggest that we meet in the lobby of the Mandarin Hotel. I arrived and managed to pick out her winning expression after surveying a panorama of Chinese women dressed in well-tailored black pantsuits. We chatted in two languages while strolling over to the American Club, where the view treated us to a show in keeping with my mission to impress her. With our hamburgers now on order—"As good as New York's?" Iris wondered aloud—she reiterated the current difficulties involved in all adoptions and confessed that she herself was so put off by these obstacles that she was rethinking her plan of going into the adoption services business.

"Isn't it precisely during such tough times as now that people really need help?" I suggested, suddenly shifting my role from petitioning parent to earnest career counselor. But my words seemed to pass her right by.

"I so miss my daughter in Beijing," she let slip, the warmth of her declaration hardly in keeping with usual Chinese reticence about showing emotion. She rebounded quickly, though. "It does make sense, you know, that the baby is looked after by my parents so I can pursue my career." She singled out her doting father for honorable mention.

As our lunch came to an end, I spontaneously placed my new friend Christine's headhunting expertise at her disposal, prompting Iris to say she would have a chat with her father about my situation. It was my hope that the hat trick of the harbor view, career counseling, and a hamburger would keep the relationship alive. As I left her, I sensed that while my banking position could ensure access to her, I suddenly feared that when the stakes became loftier, points of reference might fade away, leaving me disoriented and exposed to ambush by unforeseen obligations. At moments like these, I felt very much the disoriented foreigner.

From the American Club, I dashed over to the Conrad Hotel to keep an appointment with Joel, a Princetonian, fellow sinologist, and banker. Although the faltering Thai economy and gossip about an old mutual friend were obvious topics of conversation, they were cast aside by my preoccupation. As I recounted my chat with Iris, Joel kindly volunteered to see about a job for her at the bank, with no promises made. Flushed with gratitude, I gulped down my iced coffee and left to buy a small gift for Christine, in gratitude for her support of the adoption as well as the headhunting services I had proffered unbeknownst to her. I chose a curvy silver pin at Georg Jensen, having been dissuaded by the saleswoman from purchasing a more dramatic but angular bauble because of its bad feng shui. Although I had always dismissed such geomancy as Cantonese hocus-pocus, I was not about to take any chances. With the gift in hand, I took a taxi to Christine's office, where I immediately confessed my indiscretion of putting her at Iris's disposal. She dismissed my concern with a wave of her bangled arm, suggesting I make an even bigger splash with Iris by volunteering that only the boss herself would be doing her bidding. As she then unwrapped the gift, feigning displeasure while flashing a lovely smile, she said that she was champing at the bit to drop off a crib and baby clothes that had been worn by her daughter Kate. I graciously declined, again deferring to superstition. She assured me that the offer would stand, outlasting my nonsense.

Back at the office, I called Iris to tell her that it was only befitting for Christine herself to discuss future opportunities, and then I cannily let slip the possibility of her being interviewed for a job at the bank. She was thrilled, disarmed by the swift attention I was paying to her future. I went off to meetings in Bangkok the next morning, becalmed by the prospect of a change of scenery but humbled by the tasks before me.

During a break in the conference proceedings, as though on a mission I went to River City to locate a Buddhist amulet for luck. Straightaway, I came upon a shop with a huge display of handsome pieces, but the salesman told me that only the boss, who would return tomorrow, had the key to the case. I irrationally decided that failure to find a talisman in a timely fashion could jeopardize the arrival of Hattie. Pushing on, I soon caught sight of an artful antique stall with only two relics on display: one encased in tarnishing silver and the other in brash gold. When I expressed my preference for the understated piece, the saleswoman first tried steering me to the golden token—to no avail—and then told me to return in an hour, since both amulets were on consignment and she'd have to find out the prices from the owner. After lingering in a personal fog on the quay that overlooked the turgid river, I returned to find that the price was fine for the relic I wanted; and when I admired some coarse paper with dried flowers running through it, used for wrapping meaningful treasures, the lady generously gave me several sheets, which I was certain to use in my collages. That night I slept with the charm next to my pillow in the elegant Sukhothai Hotel.

My flight back to Hong Kong was just ahead of Typhoon Victor, which was designated the first Signal No. 9 storm—the most severe category—in fifteen years. Confined to the flat, with the rain pelting against our big windows overlooking the harbor and *The Music Man* playing in the background, I happily absorbed myself in painting. Julian and I seemed to be in parallel play as he read tarot cards, an interest dating from his childhood. But eventually, as his comments about obstacles, distractions, and surprises wafted my way, I sidled over to my soothsayer only to weave thoughts of adoption into notions suggested by the cards. Though they acted as a catalyst, much like the *I Ching*, my mind took off in unforeseen directions, finally running out of steam and shutting down.

Sensing that I was adrift, Julian suggested a contest comparing the operatic pyrotechnics of various versions of *Carmen*, an exercise we merrily called a "bake-off." Robert Preston was swiftly displaced by Risë Stevens, Grace Bumbry, Renata Scotto, and Marilyn Horne. When Marilyn Horne was singing, I recalled sitting in the Met between my mother and my old friend Jim at a performance with Marilyn Horne, a most unlikely Spanish temptress, and supper afterward at a restaurant opposite Lincoln Center, with waiters on roller skates—a recollection briefly relieving me of my preoccupation with barriers to Hattie's adoption.

Upon arriving back at the office, I found a message from Tiffany, who asked me to send $350 to cover an extraordinary handling charge requested by Beijing authorities. She did not even pretend that the charge made sense, nor did I query it, preferring to take heart in this hint of activity. As I was writing out the check, Iris phoned, telling me that I had to call her father. Despite the difficulties involved in my situation, she suggested that if he would agree to see me some help might be offered. I screwed up my courage and made the call. Mr. Xu's welcoming tone enabled me to push through my fear, but I was now operating in unknown territory. He queried my travel plans and then asked that I hold on for a moment. After several volleys of "*wei, wei, wei*" (a Chinese version of "hello, hello, hello"), he asked if I could come see him in Beijing on Thursday morning. I hastily agreed and hung up to make travel plans, immediately uneasy about the prospect of being alone on Wednesday evening in Beijing. I faxed my old friend Andy, another member of the Beijing brethren, asking if he was free for a drink. He phoned me straightaway, suggesting that he and his wife Eulalia meet me for supper. He'd pick me up in the lobby of the Jianguo Hotel.

I wondered about a gift for Mr. Xu. Beyond acknowledging the trickiness of the chore, I lionized the situation as though fatherhood depended on its selection. When I was a young banker long ago in Beijing, all it had taken was a jar of strategically offered instant coffee to do wonders, but now, in the late 1990s with China's economy booming, sights were sure to be far higher. I suddenly recalled Iris's comment that her father was a devoted grandfather, providing a clue that shifted my focus from the government official to a baby girl. I also suspected that, having served at the UN for several years, he would likely know of Tiffany & Co. Though well aware that the Chinese dislike silver, I decided to buy a sterling rattle there with intertwining rings for his granddaughter.

It was not long after my arrival at the Jianguo Hotel late Wednesday afternoon that Andy and Eulalia showed up right on time. Off we went to the Metro Café, *the* new Italian bistro in town. Managing to hide my disappointment about not going to an old haunt, I could only laugh at the effusive welcome we were given by the Hawaiian Chinese owner, whose Italian was far better than his Mandarin. I then shared my reason for visiting Beijing, realizing immediately that I could not have chosen better company. Not only did Andy and Eulalia have a newly adopted son, but Eulalia was involved in caring for orphaned children with health problems. So engaged were we in conversation that 9:00 p.m.—the appointed hour of my call to Mr. Xu—came and went. In a panic at around 9:20, I unsuccessfully tried the number on a public phone in the restaurant's entryway. Sensing alarm, Andy then escorted me out into the courtyard and dialed the number on his mobile phone, receding as soon as someone answered. Expecting my call, Mr. Xu readily agreed to meet me in the lobby of my hotel the following day for breakfast at 8:00 a.m.; he would be wearing a bright green sport shirt. I nervously blurted out that he would look more like a *hua hua gong zi* (a playboy) than a gentleman of stature, a wisecrack I immediately regretted, thinking that for such a foolish remark he might think me unfit to be a parent.

Once back at the hotel, I began reflecting on the significance of his willingness to meet me, wondering if he had found the file or if he would see me only to say no in person. I had never before felt involved in so important a matter under unfamiliar circumstances, and I just knew—yet again—that the prospect of Hattie's arrival would be riding on every nuance of this impending encounter.

In the morning, Mr. Xu and I found each other simultaneously, though I had not described my outfit. We headed for the coffee shop, where I was greeted by Xiao Zhang, once a waitress and now the manager, my use of the affectionate diminutive of her name bringing a ready smile to her face. At our table, Mr. Xu engaged me in a real workout focused on the foreign banking community in Hong Kong. I comported myself blandly, but in the full sail of desperation steered him to the China I had known before and the China I was getting to know now. He went on to regale me with tales of his time at the UN. I then talked about *my* New York, and we seemed to reach a comfortable stasis, but he gave no indication of a next step. As we were finishing breakfast, I passed across the table a stapled Chase envelope bearing his granddaughter's name in Chinese. When he then looked me in the eye with a lingering gaze, I knew I had done the right thing. He suddenly rose, and I scurried along in his wake toward the hotel's exit, whispering, "Will I be going with you?"

"Of course," he barked. "By the way, are you free for supper this evening?" I was momentarily evasive since I had planned to attend a speech to be given by my friend Christian. We had been at Princeton together and were now both in the employ of the same bank, far from the esoterica of our past philosophy seminars. That he had donated blood when my mother underwent open heart surgery years before quietly bound him to me, making it difficult for me to bow out. Then a black limo with darkened windows swept up the driveway with a *gong an ju* (public security) sticker propped up in the windshield, and we climbed inside. Mr. Xu told me about his family, speaking endearingly of his accomplished wife. Then, after giving short shrift to his son, he doted on Iris and his granddaughter, hardly sounding like a traditional Chinese patriarch.

Once at the ministry, which was north along Wangfujing, Beijing's famed shopping boulevard, we strode into a typically decrepit government building to Mr. Xu's austere but comfortable office. A tea lady immediately barged in. Mr. Xu listened to his messages, making sure I understood that one was from the wife of the former ambassador to Indonesia. I gathered I was to be impressed, but not sure why. Suddenly, Mr. Xu jumped up and opened the package I had brought for his granddaughter. While he did not recognize the intertwined rings as a rattle, he did realize that it had come from Tiffany's. I explained what it was and that the baby could happily teethe on it, with no cause for concern. He asked me what the metal was. I jokingly admonished him for thinking that I would bring his granddaughter anything but sterling, hoping that my fuss over the child would outweigh his disdain for silver. He seemed pleased with the gesture and my attendant playfulness. Abruptly excusing himself, he returned quickly wearing a dress shirt, tie, and jacket. Then, after a hesitant knock, the door swung open and in walked Madam Xiao, from the Chinese Center of Adoption Affairs, immediately given a fulsome introduction by Mr. Xu. But just as she began to lower herself into a chair he suggested a change of venue. She almost fell while awkwardly rising, and we decamped to a reception hall with enormous armchairs covered in doilies and antimacassars, tea tables, a huge landscape painting, and a Tianjin carpet whose colors and design were completely at odds with everything else in the room.

After I was deliberately seated between Mr. Xu and Madam Xiao, he began reciting a litany of flaws in the adoption process, specifying renegade agencies and multinational political problems, with the United States at the top of the list of offenders. He also complained about the $25,000 charge for a Chinese child in America, informing me that such issues would in fact be on President Jiang Zemin's agenda when he visited Washington later in the year. I mentioned that I had steered clear of the traditional American adoption route, submitting my application in Hong Kong, which I had hoped would stifle the rant. This comment, though, led him to describe the new reality awaiting me in post-handover Hong Kong. The Chinese government would be controlling the adoption process in the Special Administrative Region of Hong Kong, and Caritas would be out of the picture, especially after it had been trafficking with inappropriate entities and had managed to alienate Xin Hua, the official government news agency. Then came the coup de grace: "Caritas is a Catholic organization," asserted Mr. Xu.

But rather than diving for cover behind a declaration of my Judaism, I reckoned that my silence might just keep me out of harm's way in absurdly taking up a lance on behalf of the Vatican in a joust with the Middle Kingdom. What I did do, though, was speak highly of the guidance provided by Caritas and Bebe Chu's comfort with the organization. Rather than coming across as an advocate, though, I went on to express reservations about losing the tactical good offices of Caritas.

Once all impediments had been officiously laid out, Mr. Xu turned to Madam Xiao and asked casually about the state of my file. Like a schoolgirl keen to please her teacher, she held forth, as though I were not there. "Care was taken in its preparation, sir, but Mr. Lighte indicated his orphanage of preference. I've never come across so specific a request," she commented with indignation. "There is a real problem, too. There is no *wu fan zui* from the Hong Kong authorities." She then breezily commented, almost as an afterthought, "The file is otherwise in good order."

The missing document, the *wu fan zui*, was the verification of my *lack* of a criminal record, to which the authorities would not attest. Fearing a catch-22 situation, I was immediately put at ease when Mr. Xu swept the matter aside, declaring, "A personal statement sworn before Bebe Chu would do just fine." Then in a leap that took me by surprise, he asked, "What sort of child would you like? And why have you singled out Hangzhou as your child's hometown?"

No doubt he was expecting me to parrot the well-known saying "*Shang you tian tang, xia you su hang,*" identifying the splendor of heaven above with the cities of Suzhou and Hangzhou on earth down below. These cities had also been renowned for their stunning women who frequently became imperial concubines. For fear of making an inappropriate allusion, I explained that I already knew some children in Hong Kong who had come from Hangzhou, commenting that the baby's new life amongst kindred children might contribute to a strong sense of Chinese identity.

"But she does not have to be from Hangzhou," I added nervously, keen to back out of a Hangzhou corner and demonstrate that I was an ecumenical parent-in-waiting. "As long as the child is neither short nor Cantonese," I wittingly quipped, unable to control myself in the company of these proud northerners. I was naturally drawn to the tall people of these parts and their crisp Mandarin—I am well over six feet myself—and rather uppity about the diminutive southerners and the guttural sound of their dialect. My hosts

117

chuckled. "By the way," I continued, "my dissertation was about Yunnan," China's southwestern province, celebrated for its varied non-Han populations. "Minorities' blood might be just the thing for my new family," I opined. Both Mr. Xu and Madam Xiao immediately rejected this proposal, stating that such areas were off limits. "How about Shandong?" I offered, since it is the province of Confucius's birth and tall people. But this suggestion was dismissed without explanation.

A long pause ensued. Then Mr. Xu met my gaze and asked, "Do you want a boy or a girl?"

I stared back squarely and, after a long pause, flatly replied, "The choice is not mine. A child is going to find me," rounding out a balletic exchange with a Chinese gentleman who likely assumed I would jump at the prospect of a son, while I actually preferred a daughter. Madam Xiao piped up, holding forth on the merits of a female child, which I acknowledged with a knowing silence.

Then suddenly, as though a wand had been waved, I was given assurances that all outstanding matters had been resolved, which did not stop me from inquiring about timing. It would take about one month from that day, August 7, I was told. As an afterthought, I expressed concern about how to deal with Caritas upon my return to Hong Kong. Mr. Xu brusquely remarked that Caritas could be dealt with after a child was mine. As Mr. Xu and I then left the meeting, he insisted that his driver take me back to the hotel and told me that I should be outside my hotel at 5:30 so we could go to his favorite restaurant for supper.

Once back in my room I faxed Julian, recounting the situation. Then I contacted Freda, with whom I had studied Classical Chinese at Princeton and the wife of Christian, whose speech I would be missing that evening. Having recently spent time with them in Mongolia, I shared my adoption plans with ease. Though she could be sometimes hard to read, she was giddy with incredulity. Feigning stern disappointment, she excused me from Chris's speech.

As I was about to settle down, I caught sight of the pesky Hermès tote bag on the desk. Despite being in desperate need of a lie-down, I was soon off to Yifei's office to bring her up to date. Understanding that gratitude is best expressed in a timely fashion, I nonchalantly deposited another scarf in her outbox.

Peter's parents, Harriet Simon and Fred Juster
Lighte, New York, 1948

In Miami, 1950s

At Princeton University, 1970s

With John F. McGillicuddy, "Manny Hanny" chairman, on the Great Wall, February 1983

*With Julian in the Outer Hebrides,
summer 1992*

*Becoming Hattie's father, Hangzhou,
October 6, 1997*

Julian with Hattie in Guangzhou, October 1997

With Julian and Tillie in Luoyang, April 1999 (photo by Marybeth Mullen)

Hattie and Tillie in the bath, Barker Road, Hong Kong, 1999

Julian, Hattie, and Tillie departing Oki House, en route to the Tokyo International School, 2001

The family setting off from Cornwall Gardens for Chelsea Town Hall civil partnership ceremony, London, May 2006

Peter, Hattie, and Tillie being sworn in, with Julian in attendance, at British citizenship ceremony, Kensington Town Hall, London, November 2006

With Iris and the Honorable Xu Liugen, J. P. Morgan Chase Bank opening, Beijing, October 2007

Hattie's bas mitzvah, Tian Di Yi Jia, Beijing, February 2009 (photo by Chip Rountree)

Tillie's bas mitzvah, Zhi Zhu Temple,
Beijing, April 2010 (photo by Chip Rountree)

Tillie's virtual graduation from Barnard, Princeton, May 2020

CHAPTER NINE

Busywork

If you couldn't be loved, the next best thing was to be left alone.
—L. M. MONTGOMERY

I WAS SOON OFF on a business trip to Taiwan. The strain I felt after a day of endless visits to local banks was compounded by my having to cope with the Taiwanese accent and a ridiculously sumptuous lunchtime banquet. I was more than happy to go back to the hotel gym that evening and then stretch out and read. But a message awaited me from Rachel, my secretary, that Mr. Xu had called. In a frenzy, I scribbled a fax to her, asking that she call him first thing in the morning in Beijing to say that I would be in touch immediately after I got back to Hong Kong. I then dashed down to the front desk to send the message, offhandedly commenting to the manager that it was a shame one could not directly contact the mainland. Looking at me as though I were Rip Van Winkle, he told me I could. When I had lived in Taiwan during the early 1970s, the mere mention of the mainland could cause you to fall afoul of the Nationalist authorities. The Chinese civil war, which had ended in 1949, was still being ideologically fought by the exiled Chiang Kai-shek.

Returning to my room, I pondered Mr. Xu's news. Would I soon be on my way to Hangzhou to pick up Hattie or was she slipping beyond my grasp? When I called him, he seemed to sense my anxiety, immediately assuring me that everything was fine but that the one-month clock now had to be restarted three weeks into the process. He offered no explanation. He touched upon his postretirement uncertainty, confessing that he was interested in *mianzi* (face) and not money. I mentioned that I was aware of his impressive credentials and would be privileged to assist in identifying future opportunities. Moving on lightheartedly to prolong the discussion despite a sinking heart, I inadvertently alluded to my regular contact with Iris, which took him by surprise. After hanging up, I wanted to tell Julian what had happened, so I sent him a fax. To avoid getting wound up on the phone, I told him I'd be going right to sleep.

The next day's business obligations allowed me little time to mull over Mr. Xu's comments. By the time I got back to the hotel, a fax from Julian awaited me. He sagely observed that Iris had likely not been keeping her father informed about my efforts on her behalf and, as a result, Mr. Xu had reminded me of my obligation to his family. Julian suggested I probe Iris and send a message to Mr. Xu, assuring him that I was indeed his daughter's enthusiastic mentor. At the bottom of the page was one of Julian's madcap drawings of a bird. My laughter coupled with his wisdom enabled me to spend a calm evening.

When I called Iris, I recounted pleasurable details of my interactions with her father but let her know I had been chagrined upon discovering that he was apparently ignorant of my involvement in furthering her career. She confessed that she might have been remiss, attributing this to her own need for some distance from a suffocating father. I made sympathetic comments and left it at that. It was not long before Iris called back to assure me that her father was now *au fait* with our cordial and constructive relationship.

It was time to act. Taking my colleague up on his offer to help ease Iris's way into the bank for interviews, I prevailed upon his underlings to see her about concrete opportunities. After hastily inviting her in, several held out the promise of employment. I was buoyed by the news, but this did not spare me episodes of irrational anxiety and mood swings. It was Julian who belted me into my emotional roller coaster.

That night, August 27, the phone rang at 11:00. I dreaded the prospect of hearing Mr. Xu's voice, no doubt delivering news of yet another delay; but it was Alan, Julian's stepfather, saying that Lori, Julian's mother, had suddenly died, having collapsed in her sundrenched conservatory on a settee. This most theatrical woman could not have passed away in greater silence, thus heightening the shock. That she was a puzzlement—mercurial and wearisome, enchanting and vapid—mattered little to her son in his moment of loss. She was the parent Julian had known, and now she was gone.

I made a pot of coffee, which I proceeded to spill all over the bed, with Julian recalling that the very same thing had happened the night my father had died. We managed to laugh, despite his crippling blow, about the creation of a tradition that would now come to an abrupt end because we had run out of parents. Suddenly filleted emotionally, Julian fell facedown on a dry sliver of the blanket, his sobs startling me. The only thing that had ever made Julian weep was music. I was often caught off guard when he would turn to me at the opera, his face streaked with tears that had been brought forth at a moment in the performance seemingly mismatched to his reaction. It could also happen in our sitting room under far tamer circumstances. He could laugh and cry at the very same time.

His tears now spent, Julian asked for a scotch out on the terrace as I focused on getting him back to England as soon as possible. After calling around locally with no luck, I got in touch with my old friend Seth in New York, with Air France, who soon miraculously secured a seat to London via Copenhagen.

At dawn, Julian, my usually independent partner, asked me to take him to Kai Tak Airport. Unable to get a taxi to come up to the Peak, we took the tram down and hailed one in Central. At check-in, Julian was told that his details had already been fed into the computer; we even spotted "death emergency" in one of the fields, which did not prevent the clerk from sending the mourner on his way with "Have a nice day." As I watched him disappear into the immigration hall, memories of a past morning at the Beijing airport flooded back. Lucy, my assistant, had strong-armed a clerk into letting me on a Pan Am flight to New York after my own mother had died. That journey back home, right into a void, had frightened me. Despite secret thoughts over the years when I'd wonder what life would be like without her, that she was now gone was so disorienting I simply couldn't grasp the reality of the moment. Lori's sudden death undoubtedly compounded the complexity of Julian's relationship with his mother; and I ached for him, oddly counting myself lucky. After all, I had always known I had been loved.

Julian's departure heightened my anxiety about the adoption process. During a fitful night, the question of the baby's name again came to mind. The name Lori was now sadly eligible for consideration in keeping with the custom of naming after the dead. She had actually been called Charlotte Lorraine, but I knew that Julian did not like Charlotte, and Lori was not a proper name. Perusing the name book under the letter *C*, my eyes halted on *Clementine*. As I stared at this lovely name, its first four letters suddenly seemed to fluoresce, alerting me to Lori's initials and the first two letters of Emil (Julian's father)—C. L. + Em. Realizing that our girl now might have a new middle name, pending Julian's approval, made me hope that although Julian's parents had been problematic maybe he could take some pleasure in their benign presence in a new life. But because I was unaware of what he actually felt, I pretended to know best. Attaching memories of his absent father and distant mother to our daughter might prove problematic, I knew, but I focused on the loving intent of my gesture.

I also reverted to my habit of sleeping with the radio on. During one of the next few nights, words wafted toward me about an accident involving Princess Diana in Paris. It was reported that her current beau, the son of Harrods's owner, Mohammed el-Fayed, had been killed instantly, along with the chauffeur. The report stated she had been injured.

In the morning, I went off to a step aerobics class in Central. Emerging from the gym feeling virtuous and fit, I hopped into a taxi and soon caught a few words in Cantonese on the wireless that seemed to be about Princess Diana's accident. I just knew that she was dead. Once back in the flat, I tuned into the World Service and heard somber music. It dawned on me that Lori's death would now be overshadowed by Diana's. Of all things, darting across my mind was Prokofiev's death, which had gotten short shrift because it coincided with Stalin's.

I called Julian to take his emotional pulse and quickly sensed that Diana's death was a troublesome intrusion on his bereavement. He went on to tell me that over the weekend he and his stepfather had spent a lot of time together going through Lori's effects. "Hattie will have a fine trousseau," Julian commented. I suddenly recalled Lori's remark when she had heard about our adoption plans: "Now I have someone to leave my jewelry to." Julian finally said that he and Alan had agreed his mother would be dressed in a black suede suit. He also assured me that the turquoise charm I had sent as a souvenir of a road trip the three of us had taken in New Mexico would be placed in the pocket of her black jacket; and the glass Turkish eye I had given him for protection was in his own pocket. But the biggest news was that Julian had discovered that Lori was a full decade older than he had thought, a fact that uplifted him since her life had been longer and fuller than he had believed.

Despite the pall of Lori's death and the distraction of Diana's, I had to address Mr. Xu's needs. I recalled a comment he had made when last we spoke—that it was esteem and not money that interested him. Princeton darted across my mind, so I called my pal Carrie Gordon, head of Princeton-in-Asia, and left her a cryptic message about an unexpected opportunity. She called back that evening, and I told her of the adoption and my complex pact with Mr. Xu, suggesting his value to Princeton-in-Asia. She immediately volunteered that he could have a seat on the advisory board—their first member from the PRC. She assured me that her letter to him would not only honor him by offering him the position but would inflate my own importance to help hasten the adoption process. As if she sensed my embarrassment, she chastised me. "Not the time for it," she barked. Her sensitivity to all aspects of the matter touched me deeply. At least something with the word *Princeton* on it would be wending its way to Mr. Xu once I confirmed the plan with Carrie. Hopefully, the university itself might someday be a port of call for him, as well.

Not long after, a colleague called from the retail bank to let me know that Iris was seriously in the running for a job. "It's a pleasure to do you a favor because Iris is so capable," he commented, recounting tales of recommended deadbeats who had been in and out of his office in search of undeserved work. I was now left to mull over when to inform Mr. Xu of the Princeton-in-Asia sine-cure and Iris of a job offer. Then into the mix came an invitation to Iris's wedding in Beijing, which would stressfully coincide with the beginning of the International Monetary Fund (IMF) meet-ings in Hong Kong, for which I had serious responsibilities on behalf of the bank.

Lori's funeral was finally scheduled for the coming Wednes-day, well before Diana's rites on Saturday. Julian was now focus-ing on her eulogy and the music to be played. He sent a draft of his speech, wanting my thoughts. He talked about his father's early disappearance from the family, calling him a gentle and flawed survivor of World War II, and spoke of the difficulties experienced by Lori while going it alone in England of the 1960s, when the stigma of marriage to a foreigner had been compounded by separation from him. Add to the mix her quirky young son, who would fall asleep on the cricket pitch, far more comfortable cosseted in the solitude of his garret room listening to opera recordings. But it was his mother's words about the family car that enlivened his description of the relationship between mother and son: "I was primed for a life of occasion from the start. I remember at the age of about seven having to write a school essay about our car, a nifty car, a white Hillman Super-Minx convertible (a sort of pocket English Cadillac). 'No,' she exclaimed, 'if you look carefully you'll see it's a blend of eight parts white to one part pale blue—that's called moonstone!' She turned it into a magic charabanc, ripe for adventure, and I knew that no one else at school had the good fortune to be conveyed there in a moonstone car."

As I read on, I was never even tempted to grab for a pencil— my usual officious reflex. "Go with your right foot, sweetie," I simply replied, using Aunt Marcy's words from my own childhood to send him forthrightly on his way to bid his mother farewell.

With the prospect of adoption hovering in the wings, I felt unsettled about the prospect of leaving Hong Kong to be with Julian at the funeral. I just couldn't go. It helped when Julian mentioned he had an opportunity to visit the Isle of Iona, an enchanted spot off the west coast of Scotland—Macbeth and Duncan are buried there—at the invitation of a friend who was a street theater artist and had taken a house up there. He also mentioned the pleasure of following Wendy Hiller's northbound train journey from our favorite movie, *I Know Where I'm Going*. After making peace with staying put, I called him regularly. I was treading water solo now in the vagaries of the adoption process.

On Tuesday, September 9, Tiffany called my office, her bland tone no doubt signaling a new obstacle; immediately, I feared that Mr. Xu, carrying on a vendetta against Caritas, had introduced an unforeseen impediment to fatherhood. But I was gobsmacked when Tiffany announced, "A match has come through for you. I will fax the documents. You have five days to decide. Stand by the machine!"

Barely able to utter a response, I blurted out that I'd be up to Caritas later that afternoon. At the fax machine, I felt like a washerwoman from bygone days awaiting bed linen to work its way through a mangle. Each slowly emerging page was so gray and spotted that all I could make out at first was illegible Chinese script crammed into spaces requiring responses to questions. Then came the image of a baby. The paper was still warm to the touch, as though this child had just been born into the world, forever changing mine. Although the document still identified her as Hua Chunyun—the formulaic name given by the adoption authorities—she was now Harriet, named for my mother. Even her nickname, Hattie, agreed upon by Julian and me, took hold in this very instant. There I was, standing at a copy machine, right in the middle of the floor, becoming a father, the joy of which was being hermetically contained within me. As someone who prides himself on the continuum between inner and outer selves, never before had there been such disparity between the two, with my jubilation akin to a controlled explosion. I was touching a piece of paper that seemed alive.

As it happened, I was shortly expected at Hunan Gardens for lunch with D'Arcy, my boss from New York, along with local colleagues, David and Samir. As they approached the table, I jumped up and blurted out the news, waving Hattie's barely visible photo before them. Since none of my luncheon partners had previously known of my adoption plans, they grilled me in delight about the little girl in Hangzhou as we drank champagne and took delight in the house specialty—fish fillets with fried mince beans. Then, tipsy and full, I returned to my office, where I got news that a colleague in the bank's Operations Department in Shatin would be offering Iris a consulting position that could become permanent. On the spot, I decided I would go to Iris's wedding.

Later that afternoon at Caritas, Tiffany and Brenda each greeted me with giddy embraces. When they mentioned that I was the only one of their applicants who had obtained a match, I sensed the hand of Mr. Xu. They showed me the baby's original photograph, which commanded a very different kind of attention from the photocopy I had received back in my office. The enchantment of her face, serving as a foil for hauntingly beautiful eyes, emptied everything around me, leaving us by ourselves. Allowing myself finally to pan out—like a camera lens—from staring so closely, I took notice of her sitting in a horseshoe-back chair in front of a red background, wearing a heavy blue sweater. Had that been done to make her appear fatter, I pondered? While her documented weight was in keeping with the description on her health report—"malnourished"—the photo confused me. It was October, and she was dressed for winter. If the image were in fact current, it seemed at odds with the paperwork. I could not help but wonder about the baby's age. Had she actually been born on February 13, 1996, making her twenty months old? That image had suddenly stretched beyond its two dimensions, mysteriously dousing me in primordial love. Many matters required thought, except for one: I did not need five days to make up my mind. She was already mine.

I went from Caritas straight to Christine's office. She was thrilled by my news and suggested that we immediately make color copies of the baby's original photo. I then set off first to buy champagne and designer cookies for a celebration with my group back in Exchange Square. Though I was not sure how to explain the occasion, the story just tumbled out, with both confusion and delight registering on the faces of my local colleagues at the thought of this unmarried Caucasian holding an image of a Chinese baby that he was going to adopt.

The next day I flew to a meeting in Tokyo, where I kept sneaking glances at the baby's photo. At the session, I experienced reactions of surprise, puzzlement, and silence from incredulous colleagues with whom I shared the news. Having long been a secure outsider, I took their reactions in good cheer, always presuming kindness—not out of naiveté but rather the good fortune of experience. It never dawned on me that even as a gay foreigner adopting a Chinese baby that I might engender anything but goodwill. That night I propped Hattie's photo up against the lamp on my bedside table at the Okura, almost welcoming wakefulness so I could switch on the light and take another look. My happiness, though, was solitary since Julian was incommunicado, hopefully at peace on Iona.

Back in Hong Kong, with Iris's wedding quickly approaching, I went shopping for yet another gift at Pacific Place, choosing a romantic Lalique vase decorated with lovebirds for the bride and then a Tiffany pen for Madam Xiao, Mr. Xu's colleague at Adoption Services. At home, Jim, of all people—who had reinvented me back at Princeton—was awaiting me, on a visit from Tokyo. Aside from delivering a well-intended spiel about parenting from the mouth of a childless gay man, he was most helpful in making me realize that a whirlwind was coming. "Hattie is on her way, and she needs a room," he proclaimed. I marveled that despite the thrilling experience he was now sharing with me—a second rite of passage—my lingering regret over our failed relationship managed to weave itself right through the singular time we were spending together.

Later that day I called Alan in Chichester and asked him to relay news of the adoption to Julian if he checked in from Scotland. Then, not long after and much to my delight, Julian called from a rural phone booth. Was that the din of a waterfall in the background that I was hearing, right out of a scene from *I Know Where I'm Going?*

"How are things going?" he asked, with barely a pulse.

His lethargy caught me up short; stifling myself from a launch into news of our daughter's imminent arrival—though I was champing at the bit to do so—I deliberately focused on his loss. Though I had gotten it into my head that the coming of new life would tidily ease his way out of grief, I knew in the moment that there would be no such continuum. I suddenly found myself alone in excitement, struggling to contain myself in order to be a worthy partner.

"Who saw you off when you left Chichester? Do you have something belonging to your mother in your pocket? Are you taking long walks on Iona? Are you able to sleep?" I wittered on, trying to meet him more than halfway before tentatively mentioning the baby.

He did his best, finally inquiring about logistical matters, to which I dutifully responded, twigging that the adoption was still far less real for him than it was to me. I decided simply to be pleased that he had managed to spend time in repose between his mother's death and Hattie's arrival.

After Jim departed the next day, I began the work of transforming a halfhearted den into Hattie's nursery. I summoned my courage to call an English decorator named Janet whom Christine had recommended. She offered to come right over. After small talk and tea in our sunny sitting room, we retreated to the nursery-in-waiting, clearly in dire need of her artful wand. But what I wanted—something jolly yet tasteful, with nary a hint of a frilly chintz nightmare—immediately put me at loggerheads with the pedestrian vision Janet set forth. We finally came to a meeting of the minds involving lots of yellow.

By the time I later flopped down on the sofa at dusk, a gin and tonic in hand, Julian had called from Blackpool en route back to London, offering to come directly home, as though our previous chat had only just taken hold. I told him that as long as we remained in touch I would be fine and that his interregnum of healing need not be cut short. He then confessed that after I had told him the news about the baby, he had sobbed, torn between regret that his mother would be missing Hattie's arrival and suspicion that she would not have behaved like a grandmother. His tears were about far more than death and new life. Rather, even in the honesty of grief, he still could not trust his mother.

The next morning I met up with Christine, who offered to come with me to see Dr. Joseph Pang, her children's pediatrician, to read the baby's health report. Although the Caritas ladies had highlighted Hattie's malnutrition and I had already agreed to the adoption, it was only wise to have a doctor look at her records. Upon entering his waiting room, I was handed a form to be filled out about the new patient. "Harriet Lighte" I wrote for the first time, referring to my daughter and not my mother. I was suddenly struck, though, by the power of passing on a name. It was neither simply my daughter's name nor her grandmother's. Rather, they were now in each other's company, touching me deeply. Dr. Pang assured me that nothing seemed untoward but counseled me to bring Hattie in to see him as soon as she arrived.

It was now time to anoint a godmother. Julian and I had previously decided that Kathy, my glamorous and quirky bank colleague in London, would be a cracker of a candidate. In love with her parrot, speaker of Italian, collector of teddy bears, both a woman of the world and a hick from Frankfurt, New York, she was thrilled to be asked when I called. I liked the idea that she didn't seem maternal. What we wanted was an Auntie Mame and not a wistful spinster living out a fantasy through someone else's baby. The second call was to Myrna in New York, my cousin Harvey's unflappable wife, mother of two, and an artist who had offered to accompany me to China if the adoption ever happened. Although her willingness to help me had been delivered devoid of affect, I was never complacent, grasping the depth of her gracious interest to be involved in the creation of my family. She was not an obvious choice, a restless character within the context of her husband's family, perhaps accounting for her ironed-out emotions, which in fact made her the ideal sidekick. I had enough volatile feelings for the two of us. Without a moment's hesitation, she said, "I'll be there with a brisket," unlikely homespun words from this tall leggy blonde who hardly fit the image of a Jewish mother. The notion of a godfather was given short shrift.

Despite my looming responsibilities at the upcoming IMF meetings on September 22, I left for Beijing on September 19 to attend Iris's wedding. The next morning I was awakened at dawn by a phone call from the hyperactive father of the bride. Mr. Xu had just received a fax from Carrie Gordon inviting him to join the Princeton-in-Asia International Advisory Counsel. That news, coupled with Iris's job offer, allowed me to stand tall upon arriving at the wedding party later that day. "By the way," he asked, "can you make a brief speech at the wedding, representing foreign guests?" My usual terror triggered by such a request fizzled as I related it to the arrival of Hattie. He went on to tell me that Madam Xiao would be coming to my hotel for a meeting prior to the wedding party and I should await her in the lobby.

Well before the appointment I sat in a familiar spot where, years before, I used to write in my diary. Madam Xiao's punctual arrival vaporized all such memories. I immediately offered her breakfast in the coffee shop, but she demurred. Instead, we sat in adjoining tub chairs as she presented me with an envelope that she said was the official certificate authorizing my travel to Hangzhou to become Hattie's father. I felt like a hurdle jumper, aloft with only a few obstacles left between me and the baby perched in a horseshoe-back chair. I then put two packages on the nearby table. Her mission accomplished, and without uttering a word, she first took the small Tiffany-blue shopping bag with its wrapped pen inside and placed it in her own tote bag. She then rose, carrying, along with her Tiffany pen, a box of mooncakes in a Mandarin Hotel bag. As she purposely strode off, I followed, burdened with the heavy Lalique vase I had brought for a wedding present. When we arrived at the party, Mr. Xu greeted us, then immediately ushered me to a private room, where Iris was looking like Glinda in *The Wizard of Oz*, with the great and the good of the government along with several foreign diplomats arrayed before her. In the corner was the groom's modest Cantonese family. I was drawn to them, though my Mandarin burr and their Cantonese yowl did not mesh. After warm and awkward exchanges, I was herded back to an adjoining ballroom and ceremoniously seated by liveried ushers. There was sudden anxiety when news circulated that a minister of state was running late. It turned out that Sidney Rittenberg—a guest at my table who had spent his adult life in China, both in and out of favor with the likes of Chairman Mao and imprisoned during the Cultural Revolution—had shared a cell with the tardy politician. He was looking forward to a reunion, commenting that none of the festivities could possibly proceed in his absence. He was right. When the official finally did arrive, he entered the room attended by Mr. Xu and his wife, as well as the bride and groom.

The party was crisply staged but without any formalities relating to a marriage. Rather, the event seemed businesslike, providing gold-standard networking opportunities to an eager swarm. Yifei, Iris's pal and my interlocutor with Mr. Xu, was my luncheon partner, with the Cuban ambassador my other. She was keen to gossip about our mutual friend Selig's personal life, floating suggestive notions about his sexuality; but I wouldn't be drawn. Then, just as my evasiveness had finally been spent, the compere summoned me to deliver my remarks, which were largely anodyne comments peppered with four-character sayings—my go-to Chinese crowd pleaser. As the event at last came to a predictably abrupt end and I made my way out of the reception, I was luckily able to snare a souvenir menu, which featured a delicacy noteworthy even by my standards—braised deer knuckles.

Back in Hong Kong I was immediately thrown in at the deep end of the IMF. At dawn on September 22, I appeared in the Peacock Room at the Mandarin Hotel to take charge of the Central Bank Governors' Breakfast. Although such prominent guests were the focus of the event, it was my needy bank colleagues—sudden grandees when traveling abroad—who became so childlike that I felt cast as a nanny. Thus I was often obliged to concern myself with their well-being rather than the professional messages they would be delivering to our clients.

When finally released from my stressful babysitting duties, I returned to the office and gave Selig a ring in Beijing to bring him up to speed. After all, it had been his connection to Yifei that had brought me into Mr. Xu's orbit. When I mentioned sitting next to Yifei at the reception, he casually informed me that he had discussed my "orientation" with her. It took a moment to grasp the meaning of his words; I was incredulous that he had discussed my sexuality with her. My feelings had little to do with his betrayal of a confidence—I was not locked away in some closet—but rather with the fact that there was no way of knowing how such information might ricochet amongst those involved in the adoption process. He offhandedly dismissed my concerns as unwarranted. That he had made a career of carefully syndicating dispatches about his own sexuality—fierce in defending his right to do so—in no way informed his reaction to my distress, revealing a lack of empathy that struck me dumb. I was positively whipsawed by trying to reconcile Selig the kindly steward who had been critical to the adoption process and Selig the stranger who now showed a tin ear to my anguish. After the receiver seemed to lower itself, I began to sob, overcome by terror that the adoption might be derailed.

At home on the morning of September 25, I sat silently awaiting the arrival of Luna, our new nanny, and the movers, bearing a crib and baby furniture courtesy of Christine. Soon they all showed up, as did Christine with a cake, her young daughter Kate, and her own two nannies, Fedi and Lila. The first order of business was the assembly of the crib. After realizing that we did not have the right tools, I went across the hall to our English neighbors, Anita and David, to borrow some. They fetched them straightaway and were thrilled to learn why they were needed, happily joining the crowd, tools in hand. Tiffany, who was still in the mix when it came to logistics, then called to tell me that we would likely be traveling to Hangzhou on October 5 or 6. I immediately alerted Myrna, Hattie's godgrandmother-in-waiting, passing on information about her documentation needed for the Chinese visa that had to be obtained in Hong Kong upon her arrival from New York. Tiffany further instructed me to obtain a letter from the bank's senior country officer attesting to my employment. She also told me that I would need lots of new twenty-dollar bills. Though a banker, I was embarrassingly unsure how to do this. Since arriving in Hong Kong, I had simply used cash machines rather than jumping through annoying hoops to open a local bank account. But through connections at Merrill Lynch in New York and C. Hoare & Co. in London, I was able to stock up on crisp currency.

On September 30, Julian returned to the maelstrom awaiting him in Hong Kong; but the demands of Hattie's adoption hijacked attention, making me less watchful over him than I would have hoped. Still, no matter how distracted I might have seemed, I took profound comfort in having him again by my side. It was prudent, though, that two new fathers not appear together too soon in China for fear of jeopardizing the creation of our family. By now, his original notion of being considered our baby's godfather was nonsense. To be sure, Julian's path to fatherhood had gradually grown straighter and brighter; but it was his mother's death that catapulted him across the finish line.

That evening we followed our ritual of having "dog mess" in front of the telly—for the very last time as a childless couple. On the next day, which happened to be Rosh Hashanah eve, I met with Antony, not only my boss but a local power broker, and asked for the requisite letter and two weeks' leave. When I responded to his question about the reason for my absence, the expression on the face of this married and childless Chinese man who was seeing me off to adopt a Chinese baby changed from bewilderment to reproof. His censorious attitude carried on and caused me genuine discomfort. There was no way of knowing if he would quietly menace my career.

Even before she was in my arms, I was obliged to make the baby's travel arrangements to Washington, DC, where we were required to finalize her immigration status. Without a direct flight from Hong Kong it was necessary to obtain a transit visa through Canada; during what I had expected to be a routine procedure at the Canadian Consulate, I was subjected to an intense and disturbing interrogation by a surly clerk who questioned the appropriateness of a single man adopting a little girl. To steady myself and fight off queasiness, I held onto the counter, determined to give this cur of a bureaucrat no reason to deny my application.

Finally successful at this office, I pushed on with more chores: preparation of the paperwork for Julian's and Myrna's China tourist visas; arrangements for plane tickets from Hangzhou, Hattie's birthplace, to Guangzhou, where Hattie would be vetted at the US Consulate; and lastly, the reservation of train tickets from Guangzhou back to Hong Kong after finalization of the adoption. The death of my mentor, Professor Franz Michael, at this time was difficult to absorb. But the daunting logistics and heightened emotions swirling around the arrival of my daughter, leaching my emotional strength, did not prevent my taking heartfelt pause. After all, no matter how my way had threaded through life, it was the happenstance of this man's lecture on loess that had both cut me loose and launched me. Hopefully, the eulogy I sent back to America to be read at his memorial service adequately imparted my affection and gratitude for his introduction to China. I could never have anticipated just how intimately knotted he had become into my life and the family I was in the throes of creating.

CHAPTER TEN

Fathers

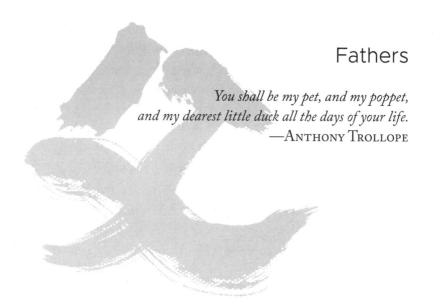

You shall be my pet, and my poppet,
and my dearest little duck all the days of your life.

—ANTHONY TROLLOPE

The night before our departure for Hangzhou, Luna, Christine and her husband, their three children, and two nannies joined Julian, Myrna, and me for supper. Late in the evening, in what seemed like a remake of the stateroom scene in *A Night at the Opera*, we piled into Hattie's room, now decked out in yellow with colorful stripes, and encircled the new black baby bag I had bought in a posh kiddie store in Pacific Place. It was the only one without bunnies and daisies all over it. There was little sleep that night, but oddly, the darkness did not linger.

At 7:50 in the morning, Sunday, October 5, Myrna and I were picked up by car. At Kai Tak Airport, Amy, an underling from Caritas—at the last moment, Tiffany was unable to come—awaited us, and we flew together. We were then met at the Hangzhou Airport by a minibus, called a "little bread bun" (*xiao mian bao*), and soon bound for the Wanghu Binguan (Lakeview Hotel). Upon finally arriving at our destination, we settled into our three rooms in anticipation of Hattie finding me, her father.

When we later came downstairs in the early evening, I asked the manager to recommend a restaurant. He suggested Zhang Sheng Ji, also mentioned in passing by a man on the minibus, which sounded just fine. There we first ordered its famed decomposing duck in a crock, followed by milky shrimp. After our feast, I expansively held forth like some all-knowing windbag, asserting that Hattie's arrival would certainly not be keeping us from sampling the local cuisine each night throughout this ancient capital. "We'll just drag her around with us," I opined, oblivious to my foolhardiness.

At 8:30 the next morning—Monday, October 6— we walked across the road from the hotel to the Ministry of Civil Affairs, the baby's whereabouts unbeknownst to us. After climbing up cement stairs in a typically dingy government building, we entered a large room lined with boxy brown sofas and a massive table crammed with fake plants at its hollowed-out center. The table was encircled by many people, and I struggled to discern the dynamics of the cast. Suddenly, I caught sight of a tiny girl and then seemed to fall into a cognitive abyss, delaying awareness of my wisp of a daughter, dressed in a yellow and white outfit, nose running, clasping a packet of biscuits in each hand and paying full attention only to them. As I reached over to Myrna to brace myself, a woman quietly volunteered that the baby's usual ration was one packet of crackers per day. While being led off for more administrative matters, I noticed Myrna sidling up to the sofa, very sensitive to my baby. I expected primordial fireworks to erupt within me; but there was no emotional surge even as I gazed at Hattie. Then I went blank. Of all things, an experience I had had at the Wailing Wall flashed before me. On my first trip to Israel to attend a wedding in the 1980s, I kept preparing myself for a poignant rush I would surely have as I stood before Judaism's most iconic site. When I finally arrived, though, I lacked the wherewithal to take in the unfathomable, and realized that being emotionally tabula rasa was the epiphany. Hattie was already holding her own against the Second Temple.

At the very moment that I was meant to become a father to my child, formalities kept me from her. Only by putting my spirit off to the side and reserving it for my girl was I able to mechanically apply my thumbprint to five documents; Hattie would later be doing the same. I was then told to write a prescribed note explaining why I wanted to adopt a baby. I dutifully promised that I would not mistreat her and added that I had always wanted to be a father. Next I paid a fee, which had to be in the local currency, heartening since monkey business was usually conducted in foreign exchange. Then I was able to approach my girl with both reverence and speed, sitting down near her. Finally, paying no mind to the possible effect a lunging giant might have on a tiny baby, I swept Hattie up in my arms, a broad gesture to which she did not even react. Of all things, I caught sight of my red watchband, which had served us well. I had held many babies, but this was *my* baby—my twenty-month-old daughter. I grew uneasy at trying to calibrate my hug about her wispy frame and was startled to notice light-colored locks feathered beneath her dark head of hair, a sign of malnutrition. No wonder she was clinging to the crackers, I thought. I sang "*Schloff Mein Faigele*" in her ear—the first lullaby my mother ever sang to me, and her mother to her— and walked out onto the balcony, pointing to the buses and trucks speeding noisily beneath us. She couldn't resist the hubbub. That she was in my arms did not seem to matter to her. Since she had likely been carried by many, she could not know that my arms would forever be around her. I figured that it was not for me to proclaim that mine was the hug of a father but something only Hattie herself could someday come to know. Getting out of the baby's way, I happily watched the traffic below upstage me, taking delight in my new daughter's amusement.

I was soon called back into the room and presented with an official document; then Myrna, Amy, and I, with babe in arms, were unceremoniously led out to a minibus for transport to the provincial authorities. I found myself in limbo, with fantasy morphing into reality. It was as if emotional rewiring were going on then and there, replacing the certainty of habit with timid self-doubt. Although I had indeed cradled babies over the years and elicited kudos as a real natural, when it came to this child of my own I was uneasy, my behavior self-aware. Hattie allowed herself to be held and looked at me only because I was unavoidably close, I reckoned. I wondered what a combination of neglect and the distracted attention of serial strangers must have been like, even though such scenarios were only as certain—or uncertain—as everything else I could imagine about Hattie's past.

The clerk awaiting us at our destination babbled on about places he had heard of in America, taking no notice of the docile child in my arms. By contrast, it was precisely because of the docile child in my arms that I could summon the willpower to appear attentive and remain cordial. After patiently pandering to his geographic interests, I was told to come back on Thursday or Friday for the official presentation of documents. By now Hattie had fallen asleep. I wondered if she did this in just anyone's arms, hoping that the next time it happened a seed of constancy might be planted in her life. This internal monologue gave way to the simple pleasure of sensing Hattie's warmth.

Back in our room, I changed Hattie's diaper and put her into Oshkosh overalls, taking great care with the yellow and white outfit she had been wearing. I handled the tiny clothes reverently and in slow motion, for they radiated import as the only physical link Hattie would ever have to her past. It was hard to know what kind of child she would become: one forever held captive by what could never be known or keen to cut free from her past, never tempted to look back. Somewhere in between was also possible. She would be the one to ignore or caress her baby clothes as she saw fit. My job was to ensure her ability to choose.

I put her down in a white enamel crib better suited to a hospital than a hotel and hovered alongside, marveling at her silence. I was finally alone with a daughter who had always seemed real to me, even when still a fantasy—an emotional version of the duality paradox now well resolved in my heart. After a while, she grabbed on to the bumblebee at her side that Julian's mother had sent months before, giving it a little shake. Then delicately stroking her forehead with my fingers, I noticed that Hattie was warm. And at that very moment of discovery, Mr. Zhang, a man who had given me advice about restaurants on the way into town from the airport, called the room. I blurted out my health concerns for the baby, and he immediately offered to come to the hotel with his wife. No sooner had I brought Myrna from her room than the Zhangs arrived and whisked us off to the pediatric hospital.

My poor little baby howled in misery while having her temperature taken indecorously at a nurse's station immediately inside the hospital's glass doors. Her sobs pierced me as none I had ever known. After being examined, she was given lots of medicine for fever and congestion, and we were sent on our way. Our party then split between two trishaws, with no taxis available. As Myrna and I clambered into one with the baby, the driver's eyes were out on stalks. He certainly earned his handsome tip for that journey, though I reckon he dined out on describing the huge foreigners bearing the tiny Chinese baby. I thanked the Zhangs and suggested getting together again to express my gratitude.

Hattie seemed to perk up quickly, soon becoming ravenous. I managed to find a banana in the hotel and added it to her cereal and soy milk. She seemed modestly gracious as she devoured the fixings, and I had even grown pleased to change her diaper, the shared moments of eye contact well worth the chore. I was smitten and started calling her Xiao Qu (Little Song, with the character Qu taken from part of the Chinese name I had given Julian) and occasionally whispering "My baby" in her ear as I carried her about. I noticed Myrna watching us with a beatific expression, unlike her usual impassive countenance at the most emotional moments. Soon Myrna said good night and retired to her room.

Now alone with my baby, who would be with me for a lifetime, I sensed memories gathering around me like guests: an ensemble of old girlfriends nodding their approval, my mother resting her elegant fingers on my shoulder, Aunt Marcy's corpulent frame hovering over the baby, my first lover, now sadly distant from my life. I even felt a twinge about my father's absence from the crowd. Though he had died years before, I still thought of him—in terms of his truancy during life rather than death—regretting that he had never been a constant to me. And there Julian was; I spotted him out of the corner of my eye, edging his way toward the crib, now very much in the frame.

Amidst this silent tumult, Hattie slept in peace. I sat beside her, stroking her tiny palm with my index finger through the slats. Though grateful that she was sleeping, I stayed by her side all night, obsessing over both her peace and her sounds. Then, as dawn suggested itself, I decided I had to demonstrate that I was a good father, vowing to have Hattie washed, fed, and dressed before Myrna and Amy knocked on our door—and I did!

In the morning, our next bureaucratic port of call was the Justice Ministry. But what began as a routine visitation swiftly deteriorated into an open-ended ordeal. I was harshly told by a functionary that original documents relating to my marital status required notarization by both the American and British consulates, the latter because of my lengthy sojourn in England. With the limp wave of a dismissive hand, he suggested that I get on a train to Shanghai to obtain the necessary signatures attesting to my bachelorhood. Managing neither to rant nor sob, I was calmly able to negotiate the British piece of this vexing assignment off the table. As for the American portion, I explained that my marital status was stated on my US tax return and that a false statement on such a document was too perilous to fathom. "Then get that notarized," he commanded. That I could retrieve evidence of my marital status from a tax return spoke volumes about my command of the reams of documents I was forever lugging about in a frayed bag. Thus, when the clerk put me on the spot I behaved like a computer on Search, rifling mentally through bank statements, brokerage reports, tax returns, a birth certificate, a driver's license, references, and police reports, managing at last to zero in on the right piece of paper. Upon leaving the office, I decided to call on Mr. Zhang, now cast as a fixer, to enlist his help.

He suggested that we meet back in the hotel's restaurant for lunch. He and his wife soon arrived, and he ordered an extravagant meal, the centerpiece of which was a whole turtle. The dish, subversively bringing to mind my old London pet, Montserrat, made me lose my appetite even before the huge turtle, bobbing up and down in a pot, had been set before us. I eased into a description of my predicament, hinting at my need for his good offices while fishing out of my pocket the name card of Madam Wang, the flunky's boss at the Ministry of Justice. With a mouth full of jellyfish from the cold plate, he grabbed the card, threw down his chopsticks, and called her, dismissing my panicked objections. He was immediately fumbling for words, his story making no sense. Then I heard a sharp click, finalizing a failed mission. Both to spare him loss of face and disguise my consternation, I briefly poked around the other dishes before paying the check, leaving my guests sucking the meat out of the turtle's carcass. Despite my hypersensitivity when it came to anything that touched upon my girl's well-being, this man's buffoonery was sure to be obvious to Madam Wang, thereby sparing us peril—I hoped.

Prior to departing from Hong Kong I had gotten in touch with an old friend, Chris Laycock, from my student days in Taiwan, who was now working at the US Consulate in Guangzhou. His reaction to my news about Hattie's adoption was merry shock. I was looking forward to a reunion and meeting his family when finalizing the baby's arrangements at his office. But now, rather than alerting him of my arrival from Hangzhou, I sent off a fax asking if he could officially attest to my marital status. He phoned back straightaway, offering to stamp everything on my tax return that didn't move and fax it right back. I then dispatched the front page of the IRS document that cited my marital status. I also called the US Consulate in Hong Kong, where Miss Mak was lovely but hopelessly vague. While speaking to her from the hotel lobby's phone booth, I was handed a document already returned from Chris, resplendent in smudged eagles and illegible signatures, with a promise of originals to follow.

Armed with this document, Amy and I returned to the Ministry of Justice and sought out Madam Wang, who expressed wonderment at our speed in addressing the matter. She opined that things just might work out, but the original would *have* to be produced before the child could be taken from Hangzhou on Friday. The gauntlet had been thrown down. The notion that I might not be able to take Hattie home was unthinkable; thus staying laser-focused on my mission was effortless. Amy remained in constant contact with Tiffany, who in turn was in touch with authorities in Beijing. Though I had been led to believe that the longstanding rivalry between the Ministries of Civil Affairs and Justice had been finally resolved, it proved not to be the case this far from the capital. As the Chinese saying goes, "Heaven is high and the emperor is far away." That I had foolishly flashed Mr. Xu's card from the victorious Ministry of Civil Affairs during my initial discussion back at the vanquished Ministry of Justice placed me in the wrong political camp, stiffening the resolve of the losing local officials to exercise spiteful and waning control.

Back at the hotel, I urged Amy to go on a walkabout in Hangzhou, and Myrna and I headed for the lobby bar, where we sipped vodka and tonics as Hattie snored loudly, fast asleep in my lap. But the real noise was to come later that evening at bath time. The tub in the room was huge and made of stone. When we filled it up and placed Hattie in it, she almost disappeared, her screams reverberating in that cave of a bathroom. "Wait until we wash her hair," Myrna flatly quipped as we soldiered on with the task. How right she was!

Later that evening, with Hattie tucked snugly in her crib, Julian called. I was so exhausted that my usual anxiety about the sound of the phone didn't kick in. Although newsy faxes had been hurtling to and fro between us, his festooned with zany animals, it was on the phone that he sounded freshly present. "Tell me what the baby looked like when you fed her the mashed banana." "How could you bear hearing Hattie cry like that in the hospital?" "I don't know about the diaper thing..." That he had barged right in with pedestrian chitchat about the baby was a heartening change. I did not feel the need to gingerly introduce the baby, yet again, before getting to the miraculous tedium. When I finished the call, I felt like he was very much with me, as I had sensed in my recent wakeful dream.

Between visits to more government offices, we managed to enjoy some downtime. At one point Myrna offhandedly asked if Hattie could walk, so I put her down on the floor; immediately she ran off, and I playfully chased her around the lobby, taking pleasure in her squeals. We later visited West Lake, my pleasure in her delightful noises diminished by the sharp metal bars of the back frame I had brought along, which was giving her a good view from atop my shoulders. We also stopped to buy Hattie some shoes. In one shop, Hattie immediately became the center of attention, with salespeople making a fuss over her. We bought lots of colorful cloth shoes stitched with animals. Hattie cared little for them but loved rummaging through the tissue paper and boxes.

On Thursday, after finally making the rounds of all the requisite offices, other than the Ministry of Justice, to gather up outstanding documents I returned to the hotel and was handed a large envelope. In it was the original tax form attesting to my marital status returned by Chris from Guangzhou. Keeping to our schedule, as though no bureaucratic hiccup had occurred, Amy and I then went to the Ministry of Justice, where I was casually handed the baby's passport. The copy of the tax form had clearly been enough; thus, I mischievously decided not to part with the original. Amy and I walked back to the hotel, feeling both relieved and smug. It was now time to relax and then prepare for the next day's early morning departure.

As we entered the lobby, we were startled by Madam Wang, who jumped out from beside the front door and sternly reminded me of my obligation to present the original tax form to her. Silently, I handed the envelope to her and asked if she might be free to join us for refreshments. She was incredulous that I had been able to comply in a timely fashion. I called Myrna up in the room and asked her to bring the baby down. We then all sat together to eat banana splits—so over-the-top they suggested maquettes of Claes Oldenburg sculptures—with Madam Wang making a big fuss over my daughter. After seeing off our tamed dragon, we collapsed in the lobby to enjoy vodka and tonic chasers.

The next morning the journey to Guangzhou was uneventful—aside from being asked in the airport how much I had paid for the baby. For new adoptive families, all roads led to the White Swan Hotel, next door to the US Consulate. Upon entering the hotel's grand lobby, which was dimly lit, I noticed that most guests with babies were circling in slow motion, as though on a surreal carousel. After we checked in, Hattie loved the ride in the glass elevator taking us aloft to our room. Julian was due from Hong Kong shortly, and we had worked out an intricate ballet for his introduction to the baby: Myrna and I would stay in my room upstairs and await his call from the lobby, then he would join us, taking cues from Hattie as she sussed him out. But there he was, already standing inside the room! So I thrust the baby into his arms and just said, "Here." So much for our contrived plan. It happened so fast that all Julian could do was gasp and clutch the baby against himself, a gesture so startlingly natural that he seemed to have surrendered to her on the spot.

"You need to take Hattie off by yourself," I urged, wanting him to catch up on the time I had already had with the baby. Of all things, the notoriously filthy and chaotic Bird Market came to mind, a venue that I knew would be right up Julian's alley. I had long ditched the torturous back frame in Hangzhou, so off they went with Hattie in his arms.

It was no wonder that, upon returning from the outing, Julian took a spill on the marble floor in the hotel lobby, capsizing as he juggled the overstuffed baby bag, a camera, and his new daughter. Watching them look at each other and share noises that excluded me, I could tell that his promotion to fatherhood had taken place during their excursion. Squalid Cantonese atmospherics at the Bird Market had been just the thing. Together, we wandered over to see the big cage in the hotel's entry hall, its frisky residents delighting Hattie, who might have thought she was now in another bird market. It was here that Hattie said her first English word: *bird*. My mind immediately darted back to that zany bird Julian had drawn at the bottom of a fax to cheer me up when I had been at an impasse in the adoption process. Then off Hattie and I went on a round of appointments at the US Consulate.

In a few days, with Hattie's Chinese passport in hand—now bearing an American stamp equivalent to a green card, paving the way for her citizenship—we were all bound for Hong Kong on the train. After passing beyond the immigration booth, I was overcome by a brand of intense relief unknown to me. Having grown myopic while going about my appointed rounds, I had not realized that the future had drawn in so close I could barely see beyond my nose. It had been a very long ordeal, and we delighted at the prospect of Hattie sleeping in her own cavernous crib that night.

We were finally home. After Hattie had been swiftly fed, bathed, and put to bed, Myrna, Julian, and I settled down to sip cocktails in the sitting room. But before there was time for chitchat we suddenly heard screaming from Hattie's room. Myrna taught by example, paying no mind to the racket, which likely gave the new fathers courage to do the same. But the noise grew gradually louder until the baby was standing in our midst. If she hadn't been screaming, we might not have even seen her. That this seventeen-pound child had managed to pull herself over the crib slats left us in awe. Then Myrna laid it on the line, saying, "Do you two want to be bastards for one night or never sleep again?"

She spared us the choice. With a casual sweep of her arm, she picked up Hattie and carried her right back into her room, with Julian and me left scampering behind. After setting Hattie down on the floor, she lowered the side of the crib, put pillows all over the room, then took the night-light—a big plastic duck—off the floor and set it on the changing table. Backing us out of the room, she shut the door, with the baby's screams following us down the hall. Myrna then announced that she was going to bed, bade us good night, and flatly said, "Over to you."

The new fathers sat stock-still in old Victorian wing chairs, the beauty of the harbor view receding as the screaming continued. Demonstrating the "Keep calm and carry on" fortitude that had gotten the English through the war, Julian finally suggested that we get ready for bed. For a while, we read—Julian, French fiction, and me, a volume of Trollope. Finally, no longer able to keep up our literary charade, we sat side by side on the edge of the bed, praying that the crying would stop. Until it did, though, Julian cared for me as I dissolved in guilt over my misguided rectitude, too weak even to cave. Though a notorious pushover, I curiously held my ground as though my future as a credible father were at stake. Luna appeared, offering to go into the baby's room and take care of things so we could get some rest. But Julian and I took the view that nighttime dramas were best left to parents—especially those who had caused them—assuring our new nanny that everything would be just fine, even though we secretly wanted her to go in and mind the baby. I shuddered at the baby's terror of being all alone in that darkened room. How could she know the door would eventually open again?

Subsequently, sudden silence became more harrowing than the screams. I got under the covers like a scared child, despite knowing that we had to go into Hattie's room and check on her. Julian immediately understood that it would be up to him to investigate the situation. Second-guessing his every move from afar, I warned him that the baby might be in front of the door so he had to take care while opening it. I heard the knob turn, jumped up, and was soon hovering over him as he crawled on all fours. When our eyes adjusted to the dark, we finally saw our girl fast asleep in the crib. Once she had realized that we would not be immediately returning, she had made sure not to sleep on the floor. I marveled at Myrna's prescience in lowering the side of the crib in anticipation of the baby's return to it. On a subsequent night, when her crying sounded particularly insincere, I opened the door and was greeted first by silence, then by Hattie happily humming to herself. She was soon asleep, and the door was never closed again.

The next day brought real drama. Hattie had left the mainland on a Chinese passport affixed with the equivalent of a green card obtained at the US Consulate in Guangzhou. But now that Hong Kong was part of the People's Republic she was granted "leave to remain" for only one week as a Chinese refugee. Fortunately, Mr. Xu had thought ahead and offered to alert local immigration authorities to our presence in Hong Kong, asking that we be granted an extension, although he could not promise the request would be honored.

We readied ourselves for battle with the bureaucrats. Luna bathed, clothed, and fed Hattie, while Julian packed the black baby bag for the ferry trip across the harbor. All I could think of was showing up at some nondescript government building in Kowloon and, without a piece of official-looking paper, pleading my case to Cantonese-speaking clerks. On this occasion, though, there was no repeat of the standoff between Hangzhou's contending ministries. Mr. Xu's clout prevailed after I patiently repeated my story in English and Mandarin, peppered with a few Cantonese quips. We were readily given an extension; and as we returned home in the prow of the ferry, enjoying the view and breeze on a humid day, I stared into my baby's eyes, incredulous yet again that I had a daughter, as she made a game of moving from my arms into the seat beside us and back again, playing her version of musical chairs. Though aware of looming trials, I simply threw my head back and laughed out loud in the middle of Victoria Harbour.

As if the Chinese adoption process had not been complicated enough, the very last piece of the puzzle—obtaining an American passport for our new baby—proved to be the most complex. While the paperwork undertaken at the US Consulate in Guangzhou had secured Hattie's right of entry into the United States, I knew it could take up to eighteen months for her to be granted a passport that would enable her to travel back to Hong Kong, where I was working. Although she could return to Hong Kong on her original Chinese passport, she would again be subject to the time limitation that had prompted our journey to Kowloon. I was clearly in denial about the daunting bureaucratic hurdles awaiting us, my optimism buoyed beyond reality.

During the lengthy period leading up to Hattie's adoption, I had done considerable legal homework, but I alone could not surmount the challenges Hattie and I were now facing. Fortunately, my cousin Judy had married an immigration lawyer practicing in Washington, DC, named Luis. He and I shared a kindred geography, having grown up in the same Bronx neighborhood. He lived in the Fish House, with its art deco masterpiece—an aquatic mosaic mural—and I, farther up the Grand Concourse, in a building with a towering doorman named Paul and its own ballroom. This childhood proximity was enough to forge an instant bond between us, and he graciously offered to act on my behalf. We soon found an arcane solution based on the concept of "expeditious naturalization," a legal remedy geared primarily to soldiers who had married foreigners abroad and were required to swiftly return to their posts overseas. It was in this farfetched context that we devised a scenario to address Hattie's immigration predicament.

When Julian, Hattie, and I ran out of time in Hong Kong, we flew to Washington, DC, landing at Dulles Airport in a snowstorm. Luis met us, with the baby's eyes fluttering in wonderment at the icy flakes and finally closing in exhaustion. We made our way cautiously to Luis and Judy's home along the slippery roads, where Judy and their two younng children—and manic dog— awaited us. Luis then brought me up to speed on our legal situation. He had been preparing a dummy file for a dry run before a sympathetic immigration officer to ensure that everything was in order. If our application were to be denied, Hattie would become a prisoner in her new country, forcing me to leave my job and stay put in America or return to Hong Kong without Julian and Hattie, the latter clearly not an option. I had not created my new family only to abandon it.

Over the next few days, Luis and I tried to anticipate bureaucratic pitfalls. Then he submitted our papers for formal processing. If Luis was notified that an interview had been scheduled, we would know the application had passed muster. That call came, and the interview went perfectly. As we were leaving, Hattie leaned over to kiss the immigration officer; Mrs. Granderson was likely the first black woman Hattie had ever seen, made more memorable by her blonde buzz cut and ornately painted fingernails. We took a photo of the occasion: Hattie is holding a tiny American flag, and I look like the wreck of the *Hesperus*.

With our mission accomplished, we took the train to New York the next day for a huge celebration to be hosted by godmother Kathy and her parrot Figaro. On the morning of the party, Hattie was ready for her debut in a gray high-tech French dress and faux-leopard Mary Janes given to her by Judy.

"Let's pop into Bloomingdale's," Julian suggested, his twinkle not lost on me. Little did he imagine that he'd be strolling through this temple of style as part of a two-father family.

Hattie jumped merrily from one checkerboard floor tile to another. As aloof makeup artists dressed in requisite black melted in her presence, the most languid one of their bunch sidled up.

"OK, dears, who belongs to that baby?" he asked, his Locust Valley lockjaw right out of a movie.

"She's ours," Hattie's fathers chimed. It took only a moment for tears to well up in the makeup artist's jaded eyes.

We even put her into a shopping bag at the perfume counter and tried swinging her around in it, but she much preferred staying flat on the floor and ducking down inside to hide from us. Later that afternoon at Kathy's house, with the party in full swing, Mr. McGillicuddy, the former chairman of the bank who had been my lead reference for adoption, swept Hattie onto his shoulders. We then stood together surrounded by applauding guests, swaying to music provided by a guitar-strumming busker our hostess had met on a subway platform earlier in the day.

Kathy's apartment was teeming with well-wishers. The net of invitations had been cast wide, as though the baby's arrival made everyone belong—and on that day everyone did. There were distant cousins, acquaintances from the bank, old lovers, a woman named Jeanne I had met on a plane in China whose green espadrilles had matched my Top-Siders, and folks I barely recognized. Today we were all held together by our tiny girl from Hangzhou, who, knee-high to her fathers, held court over a festive crowd that could barely see her.

CHAPTER ELEVEN

Drama Redux

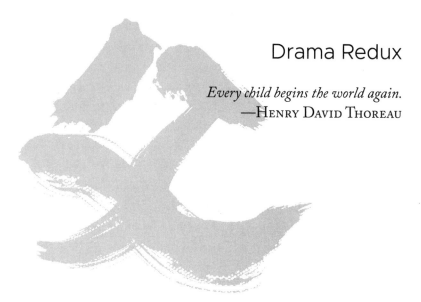

Every child begins the world again.
—HENRY DAVID THOREAU

BACK IN HONG KONG, Hattie's comfort with English seemed to track her ease within our new family. Over time I beat a retreat from speaking Chinese with her. Rather than stubbornly persisting with a language from which Hattie was clearly turning away, I desisted. It was more important for her to slot into the sound world which she heard around her rather than be part of some Mandarin fantasy I had conjured up. We took solace in knowing that only a child who had come to feel she truly belonged would tell her fathers that they were bald because the ceiling fan "blows off hairs." She had also transformed whispers of "my baby" in her ear into a new name for herself—*Mein* Baby—as we danced around the sitting room. I went about new parenting with a puzzling degree of certainty, as though I'd done it before, often confusing my own arrival at emotional milestones with those of the baby's.

Hattie's behavior spoke volumes about her parents. She gravitated toward Julian—once a reluctant father—whose ready modesty, born of both inexperience and vexation, eclipsed my lame routine as a self-styled paterfamilias. Gradually marginalized by her simple gestures of preference for him, I began to suffer silently. Bewildered by an amateur who was getting it right and struggling to conceal my own sense of rejection, I bustled about as though charitably leaving Julian and the baby to get on with relationship-building. But I was always watching, struggling to discern Julian's magical touch. One time, keen to address my demotion I homed in on a scenario: Julian often sitting on the floor alongside the baby, coolly behaving like a toddler absorbed in parallel play. A quick study, I swiftly parked myself on the other side of the coffee table that had become a hive of activity, clearly radiating an emotional neediness, which got me nowhere with Hattie. Wounded again, I withdrew, blind to the lesson being played out before me. When I finally confessed my distress to Julian, he was bemused, unable to either acknowledge my regard for his sensitivity or fathom my anguish. One evening, as I loomed above the absorbed pair on the carpet playing with pieces of a little wooden dragon, the penny finally dropped. There was no room in this family for a father to behave as though he were a victim of rivalry. The peace engendered by my epiphany was swift to take hold. Hattie became part of a balanced environment, ebbing and flowing in our home, no longer a child making choices. I was being happily cut down to size, learning how to wisely share parenthood with Julian, which Hattie had long ago acknowledged, and to grow as comfortable in the family as she had already become.

A cozy and quotidian routine settled upon our household. One spring evening in 1998, as Julian and I were watching a TV program and Hattie, now two and a half, was asleep in her crib, I decided it was time to clean out the stash of documents pertaining to the adoption process piled in a cupboard in our bedroom. I thought it best to take on the task alone, sparing Julian the busywork. With the shock of Hattie's arrival now replaced by the humdrum of constancy, Julian needed a respite from the very regimen that could never be tedious enough for me. Earlier that day our friend Ruth had taken him along to her salon for a makeover, where they had both turned themselves into blondes. His quirky dye job of remaining fuzz was just enough to remind him of the radiant chap he still was.

As I got to work on the papers, it was easy to toss out the thick sheaves that were readily identifiable. However, when it came to police reports, adoption references, fingerprint analyses, and various approvals confirming milestones along the way, I read them with care. One document in particular caught my eye because there were no copies attached; it turned out to be the crucial document produced by the American government attesting to my suitability as a parent, which led to a match with a child. I then noticed the expiration date, which was a few weeks away. Feeling alone in the room, despite Julian's presence, I gave voice to using this document again to leapfrog some early steps in a quest for Hattie's sister. My words seemed to vaporize around me, confirmed by Julian's deadpan expression and denial of peripheral vision. Though ignored by Julian and feeling completely on my own, I soon fell into a fast-forwarding daze, again overtaken by the same powerful longing for parenthood that had put Hattie in the adjoining room. In a flash, triggered by simply noticing the date on that document, I not only managed to dispatch recollection of the dramas attending Hattie's adoption but also dared to reimagine the shape of my family.

Both Julian and I were only children, but our views about growing up alone could not have been more different. While his loneliness found refuge in music, mine surrounded me as I was made to function on behalf of a mother who was ill and by relatives who had cast me as her savior. I became a master of passive aggression, seeking a life devoid of discord, often to my detriment. I had long decided that what would have made all the difference in my world was a sidekick with whom I could have shared my emotional burdens. Rather than wishing that my parents had been different, I felt the absence of a sibling had been the great flaw in my upbringing; thus the creation of my own family hinged on any child of mine not going it alone. My own longing for a lost sibling was now asserting itself, bolstered by the plausible notion that as an only child with two fathers Hattie might have a difficult time.

The next day I called my friend at the local US Consulate asking if we could begin the adoption process again, grandfathered under the document discovered the night before. He gave the go-ahead, on the condition that Caritas certify that I had always intended to adopt more than one child. I then called Tiffany, and she offered to fax me the required form to satisfy the official request. In passing, she confessed to never having understood how Caritas had suddenly been permitted to renew its adoption activities back on the mainland. My efforts with Mr. Xu on the agency's behalf would remain my secret.

Julian once had to be prodded toward the concept of fatherhood; I now had to draw him into the notion of expanding our family. Although a most natural father, he still was forever registering surprise in his new role. He seemed to take pride in confessing his inexperience, with Hattie clinging to him all the while. There was something very English about his routine—being seen as a natural amateur at the top of his game. But it was his undeniable success as Hattie's daddy that licensed me to power ahead. These two fathers, both only children, were now marching awkwardly arm-in-arm into new territory.

Familiar with the process again unfolding, I went about my business with a journeyman's efficiency, providing the required information to the appropriate local authorities. As I made the rounds, various people inquired after Hattie, taking pleasure in news about her. Just by being, she was engendering hope and showing the way ahead for a sister's arrival. After all, she had already done it; she was a pioneer! Then, as Hong Kong's summer, which overstays its welcome well into autumn, had finally run its course, an infant's file suddenly appeared. The health forms were double-sided and dim. Aside from a lengthy list of Chinese questions answered in illegible calligraphy, there were simple pre-drawn images of children with dotted lines pointing to parts of the body warranting medical attention. Nothing mattered, though, but the photograph. My new baby had a broad face with a direct gaze, instantly establishing our connection.

Early the next morning I faxed the baby's medical report to Dr. Pang. My inability to read the cryptic notation in the last category, titled *qi ta* (other), was made all the more difficult by the poor-quality foolscap that reminded me of the kind I had used back in grammar school. I requested to see him the same day because I was keen to have a chat with Caritas about next steps. His secretary called straightaway, suggesting that I drop by at 12:30 p.m. Instead of canceling my lunch with a friend, Andy, I asked him to join me on this joyous occasion, recalling the pleasure of company at lunch with surprised colleagues on the day I had received Hattie's photo.

The doctor felt that a rash he had noticed on the baby's file photograph was likely a common irritant called "widow's cap," requiring a bit of salve. He suggested that I ask Caritas to call Beijing and check with the authorities about eczema but assured me there was nothing to suggest a problem that might undermine the adoption. With medical concerns now at rest, Andy and I went to the Mandarin Coffee Shop for a celebratory lunch. I simply assumed that the "widow's cap" mentioned by the doctor alluded to the scrawl in the "other" category. Over delicious dumpling soup, Andy blurted out that his new wife was expecting a boy, further heightening our spirits.

That afternoon Tiffany was not available, but her secretary suggested that I call the next morning. I faxed over the relevant papers, along with a summary of Dr. Pang's comments, in preparation for our chat. That evening Julian and I created a little album with only two photos in it: one of Hattie and another of the new baby who was to become her sister. We had already settled on a name. Cut loose from convention since Hattie had already cornered the market with the names of late relatives, we had both been impressed by the beauty of the name Ottilie, a character in Goethe's novel *Elective Affinities*. Julian was hoping to craft an opera based on this novel, so we had long been living with its characters. We also placed a picture of Ottilie, whom we immediately called Tillie, into a frame with a playful cow on it, setting it on the dining room table so Hattie would become mindful of her sister's arrival. It was as if my own suggestions for names of Delphine and Esmé—and the playful Periwinkle—had never even been made, let alone considered. It was a pleasure to chuckle at such rejection.

The next morning Hattie took the little album with her to play school, and I went off to see Tiffany. She immediately drew my attention to an illegible SN notation and comment on a consent sheet amongst the adoption papers in the file, highlighting "special needs" and a heart problem, missed by both the doctor and me. I reflexively touched the baby's picture in my breast pocket. As though the child were already my own, her illness made her no less perfect. Tiffany advised that I again check with Dr. Pang and, if the matter turned out to be serious, bring it to Mr. Xu's attention. We would then take stock of a way forward. But I refused to countenance a hint of doubt about that little girl near my heart as I left Caritas.

Back at the office I found a message from Brenda, Tiffany's boss. Hoping for some comforting news about the baby's medical condition, I called her immediately. But what she wanted was my help in meeting with Mr. Xu during his upcoming visit to Hong Kong's refugee headquarters. That she neither knew I had gone to bat for Caritas nor that he was actually responsible for Caritas being back at work on the mainland mattered little. Although disappointed that her call had been prompted by the wish for a favor rather than information, I quietly agreed to pave her way with Mr. Xu. I then faxed the medical records again to Dr. Pang, this time drawing his attention to the section highlighted by Tiffany. The phone rang too fast. It was the doctor.

"You really need to understand what is written on that form, Peter. I am only suggesting that you know whether you will be dealing with a murmur or something more acute," the doctor coolly advised, a tone I greatly appreciated. It was as though the problem were already mine and not the baby's—and rightly so.

It then dawned on me that this health issue might actually be a ruse to expedite the procedure since a healthy baby categorized as "special needs" could be eligible for swift adoption, circumventing the reality of a second child usually taking longer. Knowing that Mr. Xu was already en route to Hong Kong, I called Madam Xiao, my contact at the Adoption Center in Beijing, but she was unavailable. I was then given a number at a bureau charged with matching procedures, but I didn't call, thinking that if Mr. Xu had a hand in presenting a healthy child as a special needs case I certainly did not want to intercede.

The weekend was mercifully relieved by Hattie's merriment in playing with Aiofe, her pal from downstairs. We set no bounds on their time together since Aiofe and her family were about to return to Ireland. Whether Hattie understood that their parting would be imminent was unclear; possibly my own vulnerability led me to project a sense of loss on her, likely a puzzlement to a child simply exhausted by two days of nonstop fun and games. On Monday, she again went to her play group, and I returned to work. While en route, I stopped in at St. John's Cathedral, where, seated in a pew—all by myself in the enormous church—I reached into my pocket and took out the baby's picture. But just holding it did us no good. I then placed the photo of the new baby in the palm of my hand and held it aloft, hoping to get us noticed by G-d.

As though finally sensing a quiver of divine attention, I then got up to leave. Suddenly, a sparrow flew into the church—a hopeful omen, I concluded, sending me on my way. Once back in Exchange Square, I tried to track down Mr. Xu but with no luck. In desperation, I called Iris, who had just returned from a trip to America. She mentioned that her father, at the Mandarin Hotel, had heard that the file of a special needs child had been sent to me and was distressed. That the child might be ill did not matter to me, though I clung to the idea that Mr. Xu was staging a stunt to hasten the adoption process. Soon he called and was contrite, saying that there was indeed something wrong with the baby and that an unhealthy child would not be a suitable sibling for Hattie. My efforts to find out the nature of the baby's illness fell on deaf ears, even as I assured him that I would be happy to take the child. But it was more than that. It was as though I had already been given the child, not by some faceless agency but by the child herself.

He could focus only on a healthy child, though, claiming incompetent staff had caused him to lose face in front of his dear friend and that only a healthy child could right the indignity and address the disappointment he insisted that I was feeling. He softly asserted that he would be personally retrieving the baby's documents when we all got together over the weekend, and, by the way, he had had a pleasant meeting with a Miss Ku from Caritas.

Only my delight with Hattie kept me from despair as she appeared the next morning looking very grown up, wearing khaki trousers and a red turtleneck shirt. Hattie and Luna went as far as the tram with me then headed up steep Plantation Road to get a taxi to the Matilda Child Development Centre. When we parted, I asked Hattie what she would be doing at school, and she replied, with a broad smile, "Playing and crying." She would dance with us that evening—with Julian to "Rodeo" and with me to a song now known simply as "Know You" ("Getting to Know You" from *The King and I*)—and just before bedtime we cringed as she neared her bookshelf, praying that she would not choose *The Cat in the Hat*, which she invariably did. I also read to her in Chinese from time to time about Lao Lang, the old wolf, which allowed me to make funny noises and get her to laugh. Lost in giggles shared with my girl, all I wanted to do was hide from Mr. Xu, the man already responsible for a miracle, but perhaps a tragedy in the making, as well.

On the Saturday of Mr. Xu's visit, Julian again had to leave. Once he departed, I had a quick look around. The picture of the three of us in a frame with little doors on it, ceremoniously kept open and in pride of place on an antique table, was swiftly hidden. I dashed into Hattie's room to fetch two substitutes: one of Mr. Xu and me at Iris's wedding and another of Mr. Xu and his granddaughter, called "Boo Boo Head" because of her red birthmark. After putting them on the antique table, I had the presence of mind to dust away the outline of the old frame with my sleeve to make it look like they'd always been there. I kept reminding myself that I was not denying Julian or living in a closet. If I had not done these things, we would not have become a two-father family. Then I noticed the red banner of congratulations that had been sent along with flowers by Caritas to my recent calligraphy exhibition. I put it away, not wanting to face the prospect of a charade—obliging me to display excessive modesty and embarrassment as Mr. Xu marveled at my being a Western calligrapher—when his mission was anything but congratulatory. From his vantage point, an intolerable wrong was being addressed; from mine, a daughter was being snatched and I could do nothing about it.

When the guests arrived, Hattie was still out with Luna. Mr. Xu ceremoniously presented me with a very heavy gift. He knew I awaited permission to open the package—a Chinese person would simply have put it to one side—and nodded, prompting me to unwrap it. I discovered inside a remarkably serene terra cotta bust with closed eyes. He explained that it was one of only two hundred replicas of a Dunhuang relic crafted when the Central Asian Buddhist enclave had been designated a World Heritage Site.

Thoughtfully, he must have recalled my visit there when trying to make amends for a situation with no remedy. Then, to enhance its value in my eyes, he mentioned that he had also given one to Regina Yip, the forbidding head of the Hong Kong security apparatus.

Hattie squealed with delight as she returned and caught sight of Mr. Xu's granddaughter. In a staged retreat, Iris took the two little girls off to the bedroom, leaving Mr. Xu and me on our own. He wanted first to tell me of his official meetings with Hong Kong's power brokers before taking a baby away from me, while I only wanted to explore the possibility of keeping that baby. In full sail, he recounted that during his local discussions he had questioned the existence of any long-term strategy for Hong Kong. He opined that Hong Kong really had no vision, and the fact that China no longer needed Hong Kong did not bode well for its future. As he came to the end of his narrative, he seemed eager for my approval, which astounded me. Genuinely impressed by his frank commentary, I forced myself to avert attention from the sad occasion, engaging him further about the local political situation.

As it happened, my boss at the bank—a local boy made good— was prominently involved in the Hong Kong government and shamefully partisan when it came to the handover. When I mentioned Antony's name, I regretted it immediately. After all, his censorious attitude about my adopting Hattie would only be heightened with the coming of a second child. My mind raced, leading me to wonder if Antony might somehow sabotage the new adoption. Forcing myself back toward rational conversation, I made the point that Antony had long been identified with local issues. Mr. Xu looked at me blankly.

"What does local mean?" he queried. "Since the handover, there has been no difference between local and the motherland. Please remember that the English did nothing for Hong Kong when it came to local governance. They are jumping up and down these days about democracy and never bothered to introduce it in one hundred and fifty years! Please," he said, raising his hand, firmly suggesting that I take such nonsense no further. With the little girls giggling in the background and our political exchange at an end, Mr. Xu rose and led me toward my dining room, as though the document on the table had some sort of homing device drawing him toward it. He sat me down and, in silence, pointed to the "Do Not Accept" box on the form then handed me an oversized pen from his breast pocket, the heft of which served to emphasize that I was involved in a rite of betrayal. He stood over me; I marked the box. I hesitated when it came to providing a reason for declining the baby. He suggested I write something about wanting a healthy child. I simply could not do that. Instead, I printed, "Heart disease," as though it were neither an objection to the adoption nor the fault of the infant. I did everything within my power to deny what I was doing.

It was in this moment that all complexities of cultural collision were laid bare before me. Although I wanted a baby and Mr. Xu wanted to grant me my wish, my acceptance of G-d's gift was at odds with the terms of the gift Mr. Xu was willing to bestow. I saw no difference between the luck of the draw in a pregnancy and the arrival of a sick child who had found me. His need for face with underlings and redemption in my eyes precluded addressing what was wrong with this sweet baby girl. I also grasped the stark reality that even if I refused to sign he would not have permitted the adoption to go forward.

After I put the signed paper in the envelope, he instructed me to write Madam Xiao's name on it. There must have been a reason for this, but it was not explained. I could only imagine that her name in my calligraphy was putting distance between Mr. Xu and this episode, obliterating his indignity and the betrayal he imagined that I was feeling. I then placed the envelope in his jacket, which rested on the back of a chair, along with an envelope containing photos of him and the little girls taken during our last get-together. His relief was palpable, crowding out my remorse.

He vowed that Hattie would only have a perfect sister, which meant very different things to each of us. The drama somehow shunted aside, we all went to lunch at the Peak Café. While walking up the path, I felt a sudden kinship with women who knew all too well the pain of losing a child unknown to them.

Getting just the right table at the restaurant on such a splendid day simply amplified my distress. When the food arrived, Hattie devoured her hot dog, french fries, "chapik" (ketchup), and ice cream, while Iris fretted about her daughter's eating habits. French fries clearly won the day, which did not make her a bad mother, I insisted. After Mr. Xu finally announced that it was time to go, I saw my guests to the tram, then skipped home with my giggling girl.

Soon Julian called and asked if the coast was clear. Upon his arrival home, he presented me with a quirky shirt covered in blue fish, something sure to perk me up. Though he knew me very well, the gesture was out of kilter. I had just given back our new baby who had never even arrived. Immediately realizing that the sorrow was not mine alone, I parceled it out rather than pretending to be buoyed by his gift. I looked at him, seeing a brand of sadness that I recognized, as if looking at my own eyes in the mirror.

The next morning we were off on an excursion. It was one of those days that seemed out of place in Hong Kong, its reasonable humidity allowing for alien clarity. Freed of mugginess, vistas stood proudly, finally separable from the haze that often bedeviled crisp vision. It was the kind of heat that allowed me to sweat gradually, the temperature affecting me over some time, rather than dousing me with a pail of stale water, as was my usual experience as I moved about Hong Kong. Tim, a lawyer I had met while wearing my banker's hat in connection with the failure of Peregrine, a high-profile financial institution, had invited us to the beach, so we piled into his convertible and set out for Shek O, a village in the southeastern section of Hong Kong Island. Simply being in that car, with Tim in his baseball cap and Julian in the back playing with Hattie in her little dark glasses, was a tonic. As we cruised along, it felt like we were passing through a stream of air rather than the exhaust of some furnace. But Shek O let us down. There was no place to park, so we pushed on to Big Wave Bay. Once beyond the noodle stands, we came upon an uncrowded cove with a vacant and pristine beach, where the sun warmed rather than blazed over the surf, offering a sense of privacy rarely experienced in Hong Kong. Hattie wasn't too sure about the sand, and Julian caught her halting steps on the camera. Finally, she began to dig tentatively and moments later happily sat in the middle of her excavation. I took off my shoes and headed for the water. Julian followed suit, with Hattie in his arms. Well beyond the damp sand of the shoreline, he happily challenged the tide, with each lap of the surf ratcheting up Hattie's giggles to squeals. They were soon joined by Tim, who grabbed one of her hands and, with exaggerated choreography, swung her above the foam. Hattie's joy not only eased my melancholy but proved shocking. Never had I experienced two such conflicting feelings in the very same moment. It dawned on me that emotional band-width is what fatherhood is all about.

Hattie's needs could not be expected to wait until my sadness had subsided. Such matters stood side by side, with Julian's emotions right there, as well. Of all places, a palpable definition of family had presented itself on a beach. It had not dawned on me to sit down with Hattie and explain that the new baby in the picture frame would not be coming. Nor did I have the vocabulary to impart such loss. Maybe it was my abiding certainty that a sister would be arriving someday that allowed her to see beyond the disappearance of the little girl's photo from the dining room table, ever assured of a happy endgame.

When the frolic fizzled out, we changed Hattie's clothes and headed for lunch at the American Club. After we settled in, Christine and her family arrived. Once Hattie had finished eating yet another hot dog, she and Christian, Christine's middle child, went off by themselves to the nearby playground, where, in an enclosed space beneath a climbing frame, they constructed their own private world out of towels.

Julian and I now found ourselves suspended between happily parenting Hattie and coping with loss. We needed some time to ourselves. Since he had never frequented my old stomping ground in Beijing and we had not been on holiday together without Hattie since her arrival, a quick trip northward seemed just the thing. The occasion would also provide an opportunity to see Mr. Xu, which was important to do since we feared a lengthy hiatus might impair the constancy of our relationship. We planned our getaway. On Boxing Day 1998, we awoke very early and played with Hattie before the taxi arrived, but I was not in a holiday spirit. The prospect of leaving our girl and seeing Mr. Xu fostered unease. While pleased that Hattie was handling things so well, I secretly yearned for a minor scene to assure me that I was indispensable.

We had charted out plans for the next few days—including visits to the Summer Palace, the Great Wall, Cow Street (hub of the Muslim Quarter), and the old Legation Quarter. While the mild weather in Hong Kong had come as a surprise, the freezing winter afternoon in Beijing shouldn't have. More a docent than Julian's partner, I took informed pride in showing him a city I oddly claimed as my own. The Summer Palace, with its sprawl of gardens, lakes, and pavilions, felt all the more grandly remote in its seasonal isolation. We began, of course, at the Marble Boat, built in the late nineteenth century with funds misappropriated from the navy by the profligate Empress Dowager. Then, after enlivening this most famous architectural folly with a bit of history, we walked down a pillared breezeway and then through covered promenades—with windows, beams, and columns artfully painted in a medley of unlikely colors that made perfect sense—but the cold finally did us in. We were saved after pushing through a heavy curtain over a doorway into the warmth of a dumpling establishment. Its atmosphere was anything but imperial; yet the dumplings in soup, with coils of fragrant steam rising too high to be real, seemed to ennoble the mean surroundings. With the racket of slurping finally spent, we sat back in warmth, readying ourselves to again brave the cold.

Back at the hotel, refreshed after a day-long respite from adoption concerns, I was with Mr. Xu—ready to carry on not where we had left off, but in a fashion that let me cope with what had happened in my dining room. I invited him for supper the following evening, and he asked me to reserve a table at Dong Lai Shur, a restaurant renowned for its *shuan yang rou* (scalded lamb hot pot). His disinterest in controlling the arrangements surprised me, casting me in a role I did not welcome.

The next morning was crystalline and bitter when Julian and I set out for the Temple of Heaven—much like the day when, as a junior professor, I had first seen it with my father, his wife, and my stepbrother and sister in 1978—now so clear that the buildings looked flat in the low winter light. The approach to the site, with its gradual passage from the pedestrian world to a sacred realm, and the fact that only emperors had made their way along this path, transformed the thrill at seeing such architectural beauty into numinous wonderment; then, while wandering about this place, we found ourselves constantly alluding to Hattie and wondering what we had spoken about before she had entered our lives. Indeed, a favorite line to people, after talking about her, was now, "Before Hattie's arrival, we used to be fascinating." Julian sometimes comically quipped that he "used to be gay," implying that Hattie's command of our attention during these early days of fatherhood had left little naughty wherewithal for the frisson of sexuality.

Next I suggested that we go to Liulichang, the city's traditional arts and antique quarter. I knew where it was, but that did not matter to our mad lady taxi driver, whose gormless look at my request ensured an adventure. She was not about to take directions from a foreigner, though she herself did not know the whereabouts of our destination despite it being one of Beijing's most charming venues. I finally insisted that she stop and ask for help. Writing out the characters, I prevailed upon an elderly gentleman, who sent us correctly on our way.

When we arrived, I took Julian straight off to Rong Bao Zhai, renowned for art supplies, wood-block prints, and paintings that had dramatically expanded since my earlier days there. It had not been easy to impart enthusiasm to Julian about this place—with its cold floors, dark cases, paintings randomly hanging along cracking walls, and reams of calligraphy paper flung on long tables. But I had experienced great pleasure here, where I had spent much time with a young assistant, Mr. Song Xuewei, who had asked that I call him Little Song, a warm diminutive. Through art, he had taught me about the aesthetics of the past, which had narrowly survived the Cultural Revolution. Had the surroundings of the gallery not been so mean, the paintings and calligraphy might never have seemed so radiant. Now, when I tentatively inquired about him at the service desk, I was thrilled to learn that he had become the manager of the establishment! Sadly, though, he was out this day, but the clerk offered to pass on my name card and fond wishes, clearly amused to hear a foreigner call the big boss by a familiar nickname born of an old acquaintanceship.

We walked toward the main north–south road, which halves the area. Once across the divide, I recalled that in this exact spot over fifteen years earlier I had come upon workmen shifting rubble— likely debris left by rampaging Red Guards during the Cultural Revolution—and digging around a scarred foundation well below street level. The lane now rebuilt, with wooden shops in various stages of restoration, left not a hint of that haphazard excavation.

The sun was setting and the temperature dropping. I grew increasingly self-conscious as I babbled while strolling, constantly conjuring up traditional society in which I had lived through books, but I was so eager to include Julian in my life that I found it difficult to change the subject. During our earlier walkabout, I had exchanged quips with the driver of a mechanized trishaw and had casually promised that when we were ready to leave he would be chosen to take us back to the hotel. And sure enough, he awaited us, so we contorted ourselves to get into his tin can on wheels, and he swiftly glided us into a chaotic lane of Beijing traffic. Julian admired the driver's bravery but was dubious about our survival. As he aimed the camera outside the protective plastic curtain, the same thought crossed both our minds: we shouted, laughing while sounding half panicked, "Hattie, we love you!"

Once we returned to the hotel, Julian and I went our separate ways. He remained behind to have supper while I went off with Mr. Xu's driver to the ministry, passing a massive construction site that ended on Wangfujing. Upon reaching the gates of Mr. Xu's compound, I was escorted upstairs to his office, where he and a friend were just wrapping up a game of Go. When we were alone, I presented him with gifts for himself and his wife. I then asked for his counsel on how to handle the tokens I had brought for Madam Zhang, his new underling at the adoption center, hoping she might be joining us so I could establish a direct relationship with her to ease future communication. But she had a meeting elsewhere, so I left the presents with him, asking that he pass them on.

Then Mr. Xu commented matter-of-factly that the head of Caritas, Joyce Chen, was in Beijing and being received by just the right people. I took this as a sign of not only the agency's true redemption but also the health of my relationship with the adoption authorities in Beijing. He shifted to a topic of greater interest to him: Li Ka-shing, the legendary Hong Kong industrialist who had started out in life making plastic flowers. "You could not have missed that new project of his on Changan Boulevard and Wangfujing on the way over here," he commented. Having already sewn up Hong Kong, Li's sights were now on China, with his opportunities further enhanced by placing himself at the disposal of Beijing's power brokers. Mr. Xu surely enjoyed watching me try to figure out the political bead game underway, which he had long ago mastered. Moving right along, he placed a call to Iris in Hong Kong, who was not at home, though Boo Boo Head was, which delighted this loving grandfather. We then went off to Dong Lai Shur, a venue that loomed large in my own life.

When I had moved to Beijing in 1982 as a reluctant banker in the company of my new boss, he had contrived a mischievous test, barking that it was up to me to arrange a dinner for thirty Bank of China officials at Dong Lai Shur. First, there was only one telephone line in the hotel. That, coupled with the distinctive *r* burr tacked onto the ends of words in Beijing and the most appalling rudeness when I did manage to get through, conspired against communication. Endless shouting of "*wei, wei, wei*" went back and forth, followed by the question "*Ni nar?*" asking, "Where are you?" Then, when I hesitated about my exact where-abouts, the line would go dead, necessitating a repeat of the entire maddening routine. Little did I know that in the Beijing of the early 1980s one was identified by a number—either a work unit or a home address—and not by momentary location. With sweat beading on my brow, I finally figured it out after begging for help from those standing near me. I gave my room number at the hotel, and the dinner finally got sorted out.

For our occasion, Mr. Xu was received at the restaurant with great ceremony, leading me to think he had a hand in the booking. His elegant wife, Madam Feng, the accomplished civil servant long seconded to the Cuban Embassy, was already seated. My presents were retrieved from his briefcase and opened as a courtesy to their foreign guest. Her gold and pearl pin and his jade cuff-links were well-received and quickly removed from sight. At this point in our relationship, gift giving faced in two directions: expressing grati-tude for a miracle and in anticipation of another. It was a pleasure. We ate in great haste, suggesting a hovering agenda. "Are you free this evening?" asked Mr. Xu, offering no context. "Of course," I replied, unknowingly accepting an invitation to a VIP fashion show. We soon bolted from Madam Feng and went off to one of the city's garish new hotels, where we were immediately ushered into an overgilded inner sanctum off the auditorium. Mr. Xu and I were suddenly flanking an elderly gentleman, none other than Mr. Wang Guangying, grand industrialist and brother of Madam Wang Guangmei, widow of China's late president, who had been left to die in a prison during the Cultural Revolution.

After our awkward photo op, Mr. Xu, basking in the limelight and emboldened by the experience, pushed us into even more prominent auditorium seats than those occupied by Mr. Wang and his entourage. The evening seemed endless, though the creativity of one Yunnanese designer was noteworthy. His designs were based on the architecture of the Forbidden City, with one particularly comical frock meant to evoke the great doors of the palace—with two brass knockers strategically placed.

As I sat in the back of the car on my way to the hotel, I was overcome by feelings of sadness and disbelief. Not only had there not been a moment for me to bring up the baby lost to me, but I myself did not make room for her in the course of this entire evening. I had played my part too well, slotting right into a very Chinese performance that left me damaged. Even so, the saga had to continue.

Little Dorrit

At fifty, I grasped the biddings of the cosmos.
—CONFUCIUS

BACK IN HONG KONG, MY SPIRITS were high, born of an immediate fix of piping-hot dumplings and the delight of recounting risible couture in Beijing. I was about to turn fifty in January 1999, by which time Confucius expected me to grasp "the biddings of the cosmos." But rather than Hattie squealing with delight at a cake ablaze with candles, I was ambushed by a surprise party, featuring an opera duo and Julian on the piano. Hattie merrily dashed about underfoot, gone before our guests could even figure out what had happened. My expression of gratitude to Julian later in the evening was silent and symbolic. Gesturing toward the nursery just down the hall—Hattie had finally crashed—I drew Julian in to marvel at the miracle of our baby asleep in her crib in a home filled with friends. No fumbling for the right words was necessary in the midst of such joyous silence. Of all things, I wondered if our own imperfect parents, hovering in the ether, were finally looking after us to secure the future of our family. Although the past could not be recast, there was much to be done about the days before us.

The next morning I was back at the bank, barely able to contain lingering elation after such a marvelous occasion. Of all things, this gay Jewish father of a Chinese baby was now cast as a stealthy poster child, off to deliver a diversity presentation to an all Chinese audience of colleagues. Then, just as I stepped into my office, with no time to savor the irony of what had just transpired, Mr. Xu called.

In an effort not to sound as though I were about to pounce in with talk about a baby, I mentioned that I had sent a senior American immigration official in his direction not only for good counsel but also to offer guidance in sorting out Iris's US immigration status. He then abruptly announced that he had the files of three children on his desk. Two were from Luoyang, born in 1998, and another from Wuhan, born a year earlier. He would soon be faxing the files and photos of the two babies from Luoyang but only the health report for the Wuhan child. He went on to say that since Madam Zhang was about to leave for a month in Japan, a sidekick, Madam Tieh, would be pleased to receive me, not so subtly advising that I pay a visit soon, when both women were still together in Beijing. He added that Madam Tieh had never been abroad and had few contacts with foreigners, circuitously suggesting that a gift from foreign parts might be just the thing. Quite frankly, cultural exhaustion kept me from trying to figure out the intent of Mr. Xu's orchestration. By this time, though, my level of trust in this gentleman allowed me to surrender and participate in the performance he felt obliged to stage.

I then called Julian and alerted him to the news. He sounded distant and confused. After all, not only had he missed this excitement the first time around, owing to his mother's death, but we had recently suffered a loss at the hands of Mr. Xu, the very man about to revisit adoption with us. I asked him to meet me for lunch. Before dashing out of the office, I grabbed the pages from the fax machine and asked my secretary to book me a flight to Beijing early the following morning.

Julian arrived looking rattled, which was hardly a surprise considering the bulletin I had unceremoniously delivered. I suggested that we eat somewhere convenient and simple since I had to race off to buy yet another gift for a Beijing lady. In a freezing Italian restaurant, I produced the files, and we quickly agreed that, though an older child might be easier for us, a younger sibling would be an easier adjustment for Hattie. Thus, we put the file of the baby from Wuhan to one side. It was tough to make out the features on one of the Luoyang children, with Julian comically commenting that the other looked like Larry, my quirky one-off of a childhood friend from Bronx Science days. Finally, we agreed to make no decision until we looked at the original files. After picking at our food, we went off to buy a gift for the woman I would be meeting the next day. In light of the approaching Lunar New Year of the Rabbit, we purchased a crystal bunny.

Back at the office, I phoned Tiffany to tell her of the morning's events and then faxed all the materials to her for review. She called back, telling me that one of the Luoyang babies was a boy. With the older child eliminated and one of the Luoyang children a boy—Julian and I had long before agreed that it might be tough for a little boy to have two fathers—it looked like the child we couldn't even see well might be coming our way. I was uncomfortable with the element of choice being introduced into what I regarded as a godly process and continued to long for the child I had been denied, still mourning her loss and incapable of articulating my grief. After a sleepless night, I was again bound for Beijing.

Mr. Xu's driver left me in front of the ministry at 2:30, where he was awaiting me on the steps. Placing his hand on my shoulder, he told me that Madam Tieh was expecting me at another venue where adoption files were kept and matches made. It was rare for a foreigner to be admitted there, he confided, and I expressed my astonishment and gratitude. I reckoned that any queries about the child whose face I could not make out on the photo would be answered there.

I was shortly taken to a fortress-like building near Tiananmen Square, where I was obviously expected. In the lobby, the sound of clacking heels growing louder alerted me to Madam Tieh's hurried approach. I then did everything I could to put her at ease, assuring her that a brief delay caused, no doubt, by a sense of responsibility for her worthy work, would hardly put her under the gun. With a sigh of relief, she smiled, and we walked to her office, a dimly lit cavern, its shelves stacked with vertiginous towers of manila files, reminiscent of the Circumlocution Office in *Little Dorrit*—worlds away, one would think, from China. I was shown to a chair next to Madam Tieh's desk, where she pushed a pile of papers in my direction, assuring me that these files had been personally vetted under the supervision of Mr. Xu and that amongst them there was sure to be a child to my liking. I quietly set down between us the bag holding the crystal rabbit, which silently vanished in moments.

As I opened the files, I felt confronted by each face, which not only stared back but seemed to advance toward me, pleading for me to make them my own. The task did not get easier as I plunged deeper into the pile. Based on likely random criteria that I could not fathom, I winnowed out a few possible children and brought them to Madam Tieh's attention. With jarring immediacy, she picked up the phone and put calls through to various orphanages, making it clear that her inquiries were high priority and eliciting frank comments about the children. Her conversations over, she suggested that I keep looking, leading me to believe that no child had so far been identified as noteworthy. I returned to the files and began reading again. One caught my eye because I could not get a good look at her, as she must have moved her head when the photo was taken.

"What about this little girl with the quirky photo in the file I just read?" I asked.

Torn between putting up with me and demonstrating her esteem for me, Madam Tieh sounded nonchalant. "Sure, Dr. Lighte," she agreed, the rare use of my title both jarring and embarrassing. Clearly, mention of my PhD had been passed on to her by Mr. Xu to dignify this intruder. "Let's take a look. She might well be worth considering. I'll call the Luoyang orphanage. She's a good age, too, born in February 1998."

It dawned on me that this might be the same child Julian and I had puzzled over in the frigid Italian restaurant. Then suddenly I caught sight of a teetering pile of files off in a corner of the room, which toppled over in slow motion. A nonchalant clerk then ambled over and gathered them up in a haphazard fashion, paying little attention to what he was doing. I wondered if photos and documents were now being randomly shuffled into the wrong sleeves, disconnecting these children from the scant tidbits of their backgrounds. Like some dark cartoon, the room now seemed to be filling up with a crowd of displaced babies whose crawling bodies passed through each other, moving about in no particular direction over my feet. Feeling trapped, I grew nauseated amidst this throng of children on the scuffed linoleum floor beneath me. I had to escape. Suddenly I stood up and said, "I would be pleased to leave the selection of a baby to you and Mr. Xu." Barely managing a farewell in keeping with Madam Tieh's station and kindness, I raced out to Mr. Xu's car, where I could not recede far enough into the seat's plush upholstery to ensure that my muffled sobs were kept from the driver.

Hardly in Hong Kong long enough to play with the baby I already had, I was soon bound for Singapore to attend a regional meeting. It took all my powers even to appear present—let alone engaged—so oppressed was I by trying to fathom how my baby would ever find her way out of that warren of files in Beijing to complete my family. During a session chaired by my boss that could have been about anything, a hand suddenly dropped a pink message slip atop my pad of Chinese doodling; I was to call Mr. Xu ASAP. The optics were perfect for me to excuse myself on urgent bank business, although just about everyone who could crack the whip was around that table. Immediately outside the door, my saunter turned into a sprint. Back in my hotel room, I called Mr. Xu, who told me that he had finally chosen a child for me himself and that an envelope was on its way to Hong Kong; I could not make out if he called the baby Xiao Ai or Xiao Hai. I returned to the meeting, trying hard to soldier on despite this news.

Not long afterward I was again in Hong Kong, anticipating a fitful night caused by the uncertainty of the envelope's arrival. But I was greeted at the door by Julian, who was holding Hattie in one arm and an envelope in the other, telling me that three files had been sent by Mr. Xu for our perusal. Now in my arms, Hattie declared, "Papa come back," her usual disarming greeting of welcome after one of my trips. We all went to the dining room table, where I produced a small doll dressed in a brightly colored folksy outfit that engrossed her immediately, allowing Julian and me time to pore over the papers from Beijing that would forever change the dynamics of our family. Exhilaration was tempered by the dread of choice. I didn't want to play G-d; I just wanted G-d to give me a baby—the way it worked with everyone else.

Looking at the three files, we noticed a black checkmark in the upper left-hand corner on a photo of a baby named Xiao Hai, who turned out to be the child from Luoyang, born in February 1998, whom I had not been able to make out clearly! This time, though, a baby's round face looked right back at me. She was dressed in a green-and-white checkered jacket and padded red-patterned leggings tied with red ribbons around the ankles, and stuffed into a green high chair in front of a homespun mural hinting at a pastoral English scene—with a pagoda thrown in.

The next morning, with Hattie's February birthday approaching, my first order of business was to order human-sized blow-up bunnies for her party the following Saturday. I had heard about a factory that supplied such novelties to film studios in the States.

The New Year of the Rabbit celebration, roughly coinciding with Hattie's big day, begged for such fun. After a comically serious phone conversation with a clerk in some distant factory, I composed myself to call Madam Tieh to discuss our new daughter. With Mr. Xu's imprimatur mercifully sparing us the need to choose, I told her of our delight with Xiao Hai. But she could not get enough assurance of my satisfaction with her efforts on my behalf. Running out of ways to express my gratitude, I finally said that immediately after speaking to her I would call Mr. Xu and sing her praises. She caught her breath and was becalmed, at last accepting my kudos for her job well done. I did just as I had promised, but Mr. Xu barely paid lip service to my compliments about Madam Tieh. He grew philosophical about my now becoming the father of a second child, steering the conversation in an unforeseen direction.

"I've lived through the era of the one-child policy. Can you believe that some people now say they wouldn't have more children? For the life of me, I simply can't fathom anyone wanting only one child. By the way, I just knew that you would want a second child," he said, imparting intimate prescience about my family.

I learned that he had a son, though he had only mentioned his daughter and granddaughter, more in keeping with the narrative of a Western family man than a typical Chinese father's obsession with his sons. Owing to my own trope on Freudian parenting, I got it in my head that little girls never dislike their daddies.

The formal approval to adopt Xiao Hai soon arrived. I then noticed on the underlying documentation that the baby's home province was incorrectly romanized—spelled "Hunan" rather than Henan. Then I was alerted to the words *bu liang*, meaning malnourished. Since there was clearly a disconnect between such a pronouncement and the robust little girl sitting in the high chair, I decided that the comment identifying her as having "special needs" was in fact a ruse contrived by Mr. Xu for me to jump the queue in adopting a second child. Considering Mr. Xu's apparent approval of that checkmark on Xiao Hai's photo, I found it inconceivable that he might have either overlooked or sanctioned an adoption duplicating the recent sad tale that took a baby from me. His blessing of this match unleashed joy at the possibility for the new adoption but also renewed profound longing for the child I had lost. I never knew one could celebrate and mourn in the very same moment.

I found myself learning that feelings were not a matter of Manichaean alternatives. A new brand of uneasy joy was escorting me into a world of emotional variety. I probably still sounded the same—opinionated and brusque—but I was undergoing profound change well beneath the surface, as though baffles were coming down, freeing me from confines long stifling my emotional breadth. I was now awash in solace and at home in a new spiritual place. Experiencing a gratifying awareness of my responsibility, no longer was I the burdened child in my mother's imperfect life. Awareness alone had never helped me shed that millstone. It took the coming of a child, the loss of a child, and the coming of another to recalibrate my psychological coordinates.

It was time to alert Luis, our cousin and lawyer in Washington, that Tillie was on the way. Mindful of his loving and successful stewardship of Hattie's expeditious naturalization, we assumed he would do the same for the new baby. Several months before, I had received cryptic vibes from my uncle that I had somehow fallen afoul of Luis, his son-in-law. But rather than attempt a forensic analysis of receding memories, I simply wrote to Luis, reiterating my gratitude to him, assuming blanket responsibility for anything I might have done to offend him, and assuring him that he would be forever associated with the magic of my family's creation. Receiving no response, I reckoned that my message of contrition had undoubtedly cleared the air.

Now buoyed by a sense of false well-being, I faxed Luis. The chill of his response—a terse refusal to act on our behalf— stunned me. He suggested another lawyer who could be brought up to speed if I first wired a retainer. Here I was, doing everything in my power to create a family only to have my mission mysteriously subverted by a relative. If only I had known then that my future daughter had become collateral damage born of Luis's failing marriage to my cousin Judy.

I was too wounded to reply and immediately sought advice from Mimi, my local trust lawyer. She steered me to some American attorneys in out-of-the-way places, where they could most likely focus on our story with undistracted and sympathetic immigration officials well known to them. But one lawyer in Hawaii was unable to focus on our tale, assuring me with neither confidence nor conviction that all would be just fine, while another in rural Colorado was more interested in the details of Hong Kong nightlife than the baby's immigration status. After several further conversations, I found my way to Susan Bierenbaum in Los Angeles—hardly a remote area, as suggested—who seemed to hold my hand with firm warmth even from afar, telling me of her superb relations with local immigration authorities, stating declaratively that the baby would get her passport in a timely fashion.

On Friday, it was a relief for Julian and me to head over to the Matilda Child Development Centre, where Hattie would be celebrating her birthday with school friends. Arriving with a cake covered in bunnies, we watched our girl playing with her pal Min Min, delighting in her role as a jolly companion for the towering Filipina, who had Down syndrome. The Matilda school had seemed a natural port of call for Hattie. My own memories of P.S. 90 in New York, where children with visual and other disabilities shared the building with us, had informed our decision. Amidst the lively festivities, we mentioned to Hattie's teacher that another baby was on the way. She suggested that we sign her up on the spot, and we did. Later that afternoon Hattie arrived home with chocolate on her shoes, testimony to the success of her birthday party. But this was only a warm-up for the bigger occasion the following day.

The next morning Hattie received her first birthday present from Luna: Barbie sneakers. Our nanny recounted that when she and Hattie had been in Central one afternoon and wandered into a shoe store, Hattie had spotted a pair and tried to steal them. Now in her pajamas and new sneakers, Hattie opened an enormous box that had come from our friends, the Finnertys, in Australia. She was soon dressed in a kangaroo costume. The bell sounded from the lobby, signaling delivery of the inflatable bunnies. I took the elevator down and was greeted by a surreal crowd scene: fifteen blown-up rabbits—nearly my height!—their paws weighted down so they appeared to be waiting patiently for the elevator to take them to the sixth floor.

With my laughter greeted by a po-faced delivery man simply doing his job, I began ushering the varmints into the elevator. Once filled, I called Julian on the intercom, matter-of-factly alerting him to their arrival; I then took the stairs. By the time I reached our flat, it looked like a scene out of a deliberately comical version of the 1970s horror film *Night of the Lepus*. Hattie was nowhere to be seen, though I could hear her giggles from within the crowd. Aside from featuring the rabbits, we had also engaged the services of a woman named Annie, who would later craft animals made of dough for the children. The party was a great hit, our joy enhanced all the more as we stood on the terrace and watched Hattie's guests down below walking hand in hand with bobbing rabbits at their sides.

Since Hattie's birthday coincided with the Chinese New Year season, we made our pilgrimage to Victoria Park to seek out yellow precious things, those exotic branches festooned with nature's version of blown-up rubber gloves. Once back home, our mission accomplished, Hattie still had birthday presents to open, with Hungry Hippos the hit of the day. I wanted time to pass slowly, as Julian would be going to London later that evening and I dreaded the prospect of coping with the drama of a new lawyer on my own. I suddenly had an anxious sense of what it might be like as a single parent. I regained my buoyancy, though, after Hattie took the bait for a new tricycle, an idea planted after friends had suggested that we present her with a special gift from her sister upon the baby's arrival from China. Instead of watching the fireworks that night, we danced around to Juanita Hall singing "Happy Talk," which swiftly morphed into "Hattie Talk." I was coming to understand the depth of Hattie's magic, realizing that my efforts on her behalf helped me look after myself, and that my own well-being was increasingly enhanced the closer we grew to each other. It was not simply becoming a parent that was reorienting me; rather, it was as though Julian and I had leapt off moving parallel sidewalks, beckoned onto a third that we were now sharing with Hattie. Parenthood was a revolutionary matter—a paradigm shift eliciting sunny surrender.

I caught myself often glancing at photographs of Hattie with Julian and me, as though objective evidence were required to steady my sense of evolving reality. That I was in love with my family did not protect me from bouts of emotional disorientation. I came to rely on our photographs as confirmation of the real life before me—a static and two-dimensional proof of its reality. My dream had come true, but at times I was just uneasy.

One day after the bunnies had been dispatched and Julian was on an extended visit to England, I entered the flat after work and was struck by the silence. There were no accelerating baby steps coming my way, nor sounds of Hattie's inevitable defiance of Luna. I trod lightly, moving forward like an errant teenager coming in after curfew. When I peeked into the kitchen, I saw Luna, looking toward the washing machine, with Hattie on its top both still and blank. As I gingerly approached her, she seemed torn between wanting me to come closer and not to come closer.

"Hattie jumped from the top bunk bed in the back room and hurt her leg," Luna haltingly recounted, as though expecting to be reprimanded for a mishap on her watch. Observing closely how Hattie seemed coiled around her oddly folded limb, I knew it must be broken. Then, noticing that Luna was cowering, I assured her that accidents happen. She brightened with what she took as absolution, and we immediately arranged to take Hattie to the Adventist Hospital. Rather than dealing with the uncertainty of a local taxi, Luna called Christine's nanny, who swiftly appeared in an enormous old station wagon. I approached Hattie like a forklift, bending my knees and raising her into my rigidly outstretched arms.

Our wait for the pediatric orthopedist, Dr. Hsu, seemed endless. When at last he appeared and took Hattie from me, I followed closely behind, our eyes locking as we passed into the examination room. I asked Luna to come along in case the doctor had any detailed questions about the fall itself.

"Is the servant trustworthy?' the doctor asked.

"Your question is inappropriate. Do care for my daughter," I coolly instructed. I then pivoted toward Luna to offer a fulsome apology and gently asked her to wait for us in the anteroom, sparing her further affront.

"I can never fathom why you Americans care so much about servants. If you were English, you would understand," the doctor confided, explaining that he had been educated in the UK.

I couldn't summon the strength to deliver my speech about being a small "d" democrat and how I always felt awkward and guilty when dealing with people in my employ. I hovered over Hattie, assuring her that I would shortly be swooping her up, then letting my arms swing comically as I did a little dance, looking like the scarecrow from *The Wizard of Oz*.

The break was straightforward, warranting a cast for eight weeks. Hattie perked up as she carefully watched her leg being wrapped, amazed by the immobilizing plaster quickly warming and hardening.

Once back home late that night, I noticed Mr. Xu had faxed a drawing of a pair of little rabbits, with a colophon stating, "Two is good." My new yet distant daughter was suddenly with us in the house. With a smile and tears, I then took Hattie into bed with me, surrounding her with mountains of pillows. Before going to sleep, I told her we had to first paint a star on her cast. She chose green, and I stenciled on the shape, filling it in with watercolor, much to her delight. As we later lay sleeping, she must have swung her leg in my direction and hit me in the head. Despite the sudden pain waking me with a start, I managed to burst out laughing in the darkness, quickly taking care not to awaken her.

Hattie was thrilled to demonstrate her new method for crawling about, dragging her immobile leg behind her—the cast now decorated with more stars, each a different color. Soon over the shock of the accident, Hattie began cheering me up, as though sensing that I remained shaken by her delicacy. I also found myself taking orders from her as we went out in the stroller for walks, and corrected on many occasions when it came to directions and destinations. While at home, I had taken pains to be breezy with Luna, showing not an inkling of distrust in her—nor had Hattie's usual indifference toward her changed, which I took as an endorsement of my feeling that the nanny had simply been an innocent bystander to an accident. Quickly becoming an intruder on my girl's routine, I knew she was on the mend.

I was distracted at the office and made it clear that I was unavailable for travel. Of all things, it was time for the periodic change of my computer password. I perked up, though, by using the new baby's name, typing in "OTTILIE8" (eight is a lucky number in China), which was rejected. Taking this in stride rather than as a bad omen, I substituted a nine, and from that moment on her name greeted me every morning. But we still had to sort out her middle names. Julian's late mother remained in the mix. Since her departure from Julian's life prior to his becoming a father had put distance between them, he allowed consideration of her name. Her given name, Charlotte, was one he didn't fancy; her nickname, Lori—not acceptable—stood for Lorraine, her middle name, which seemed fine. Since Hattie had two middle names, we wanted yet another. Though Goethe's Ottilie had been no heroine, Uncle Bernard, my father's handicapped brother of true gravitas, seemed a namesake of worthy sway. Now that I was on the prowl for a *B* for Bernard, my mother's great friend Beata came to mind. They had met in a hospital, where both were recovering from nervous breakdowns resulting from failed marriages. A German émigré whose accent had delighted me as a child, she worked at the *New Yorker* and was a world traveler whose tales of Pakistan's Hunza Valley had captured my childhood imagination.

With middle names now settled, there remained the issue of a Hebrew name. After doing a bit of research, I chose Brucha, meaning blessing, a name that transposed Uncle Bernard's Hebrew name into a feminine version. This was a pleasurable workout compared to the selection of Hattie's Hebrew name. She seemed destined to be called Yita, my mother's name. That left only the choice of our new baby's Chinese moniker. I dove into my dictionary for several days. Julian alternated between uh-huhs and silences as I banged on, trying to involve him in the esoterica of radicals, homophones, and the beauty of traditional characters.

His indifference, though, did not halt my monologue. After all, Julian had long been holding forth on Rimsky-Korsakov and other Russian composers near and dear to him. Knowing each other so well, we suddenly burst out laughing without having to remind each other what bores we both were. Then, as though following a drum roll, I shared the outcome of my deliberations with him: the character *ti*, combining the strong qualities of femininity, with the verb "to be," meaning "enchantingly beautiful." Ottilie Lorraine Beata, known by the affectionate diminutive Xiao Ti, would be joining Harriet Marcella Clementine—Xiao Qu. Finally, as though my linguistic contortions had given him license, he welcomed his late mother into our family. "Lorraine sounds lovely," he mused.

Soon Tiffany called, urging me to be in touch with a Mr. Pei, the head of the orphanage in Luoyang, who had been put on alert by authorities in Beijing—no doubt the handiwork of Mr. Xu. He could not have been more welcoming, speaking warmly of the baby's loveliness but also confiding that she did not yet walk. I processed the latter bit of information as good news, seeing things from Hattie's vantage point: her sister would not yet be upright, thereby establishing an unchallenging pecking order.

I was now in regular communication with our new lawyer, who would be handling the baby's expeditious naturalization. Buoyed by Susan's infectious confidence, I called my cousin Billy in Los Angeles, who immediately invited us to stay with his family when we came to sort out Tillie's passport; but his hospitality was sure to engender intrigue, I feared, since Luis, our lawyer who had abandoned us, was his brother-in-law. But Billy would hear nothing of my qualms, insisting that we stay with him, his wife Patty, and their two young daughters.

On the home front, Hattie was clearly aware of a tsunami in the offing. Suddenly, she was staking out the world around her.

"Where my stroller?" she demanded, keeping it close by, though she was not leaving the house. She suddenly started worrying about her clean clothes, as though taking inventory. "Red one, where?" she asked, opening her drawer and expressing concern that laundry might be missing. That she wasn't tall enough to see into the drawer mattered little; nor did our showing her the piece of clothing she feared had gone amiss reassure her. Her disorientation had been compounded by Julian's return from England after a lengthy absence. In order to obtain a proper Hong Kong visa, he had to be away for three months. Not only was a sibling soon to arrive, but Hattie had to be gradually reintroduced to Julian. Even I was off kilter, having awkwardly adjusted to going it alone with Hattie. In need of some time with Julian, once Hattie was down for her afternoon nap I decided to go with him to buy the pink tricycle that would arrive as a gift along with the new baby. Our mission accomplished in Kowloon, we stashed it behind the hall stairs. We kept Hattie close to us, lavishing affection on her, hopefully insulating her from the drama of the new baby's arrival.

In the midst of this hubbub, I was obliged to fly to New York to discuss yet more management changes within the bank. While there, I was happily able to see Mr. McGillicuddy, my mentor and reference for Hattie's adoption, and fill him in on my growing family. I carved out time as well for Marybeth, Ottilie's anointed godmother, a Diane Keaton doppelgänger who would be joining us on the trip to China. She immediately told me that her mother had gone to Mass and prayed to Saint Joseph, the patron saint of fathers, for us. Marybeth and I had met long before on my first day at the bank, when I had nervously stood in her presence. She had gestured for me to be seated where there was no chair, so I perched on an overturned rubbish bin. In time, I had gotten to know her old-fashioned Irish Catholic family, learning of her grandmother who said prayers for Elvis Presley and disapproved of the Kennedys. Marybeth was a spirit of rectitude swathed in elegance and giggles, which made for a valued presence in my life. I always took delight in her many roles; she could dress to the nines, discuss the restructuring of Filipino debt, relate comical stories about her ancient aunt and uncle in Astoria, and sit on the floor to play with babies—all at the same time. We could not have chosen a better role model for our new daughter.

Time was now growing short before the trip to Luoyang to get Tillie, with those familiar, though no less overwhelming, tasks awaiting me back in Hong Kong. Aside from having to make provisions for my absence from the bank, I had to have tickets for the baby's departure from Hong Kong for the States so that she could be admitted back into Hong Kong from the mainland, make arrangements for Marybeth's visa to China, obtain a letter from the US Consulate to ensure that the baby's entry into America would be in keeping with the expeditious naturalization process, and obtain a document from the bank attesting to my employment. Booked on a direct flight to Los Angeles, I was now spared the possibility of another unpleasant encounter at the Canadian Consulate over a transit visa for the baby. We again decided that traveling up to China together would be unwise, but the rationale had changed. While we were still wary of falling afoul of authorities as a gay couple daring to adopt a baby, it was Hattie's well-being that commanded our attention. Julian stayed behind to spend as much time with her as possible before joining me once the new baby was in my arms. Our sexuality was triumphing, by both dignifying and subverting the ultimate bourgeois institution—the family.

CHAPTER THIRTEEN

Passover and Maundy Thursday in Luoyang

Do you have déjà vu, Mrs. Lancaster?
I don't think so, but I could check with the kitchen.
—HAROLD RAMIS AND DANNY RUBIN, FROM *GROUNDHOG DAY*

On the day of the journey in late March 1999, I returned from the office late in the morning, having tended to loose ends. I was determined to leave things in good order, as best I could, knowing full well that my censorious Chinese boss's disapproval was only compounded by my adoption of a second child. Then Julian, Marybeth, Hattie, and I ventured up the steep path to the Peak Café for lunch. Hattie was both comical and anxious as she babbled about the coming of the baby, alerting us to her distress. We held her tight, showering kisses on our child who was about to become an elder sister. Skipping back down the hill made for much giggling, which was cut short by our discovery that the water had been turned off in our building, prompting Marybeth to comment that she would have to visit China to take a bath. I dug out the spool of red ribbon I had bought prior to my trip to get Hattie and again tied pieces to everyone's luggage for spiritual protection. Of course, my watch with its red band was on my wrist. We then presented Marybeth with a small Fabergé-like egg, officially recognizing her as the new baby's godmother.

Everyone came down to see Marybeth and me off to the airport, where my friend Tim and Amy from Caritas would be waiting. While Julian and I saw no reason for godfathers, when Tim, who had witnessed Hattie's discovery of sand back on that Hong Kong beach, expressed interest in coming along, we readily invited him. While meeting at the China Southern Airlines check-in counter, I presented him with a silver and mother of pearl magnifying glass, welcoming his participation in the occasion.

There were no flights to Luoyang, so we flew to Zhengzhou, a dreary industrial city I had visited on my first trip to China in 1978. As we entered the arrival hall, I spotted a placard bearing the baby's institutional Chinese name: Dang Xiaohai. A gentleman emerged from behind it and came toward me, introducing himself as Mr. Pei, the man I had spoken to at the orphanage. He had come personally to greet me, with two cars awaiting us outside the airport's doors. I was readily put at ease by Mr. Pei, whose graciousness went beyond his statement that it was his pleasure to be at my disposal—on Mr. Xu's behalf.

Soon we were bound for Luoyang, one of China's ancient capitals, renowned for its peonies. The story goes that in the seventh century the Empress Wu, ensconced in her capital at present-day Xian, had decreed that all flowers in her garden were obliged to bloom in the winter. Banished for its defiance, the peony was dispatched to Luoyang, where it has thrived ever since. Tim, politely listening to me talk about flowers in history, had the misfortune of sitting behind the driver, who suddenly opened his window and spat. Fortunately, Tim closed his window just in time to spare himself a spittle shower. It was a tedious drive, punctuated by a fight at a tollbooth, into which a driver careened, pummeling the attending official. After we arrived at the Peony Hotel, Mr. Pei told us he would be back tomorrow morning at 8:30 with my daughter and took his leave.

The next day, April Fool's Day, which that year coincided with the first day of Passover and Maundy Thursday, we gathered in the lobby at the appointed hour to await the arrival of Mr. Pei and the baby. A minivan soon pulled up the drive, and a frisky woman alighted holding a bottle in her hand, followed by a man carrying the baby, her tiny hand flopping at her side. When I finally caught sight of the perfect face of my spirited bobbing poppet, my very being was again instantly rearranged. Hattie had made me a father, and Tillie now took her rightful place comfortably in my newly spacious heart—two miracles wrought by little baby girls.

Mr. Pei quietly counseled that I speak not a word of Chinese in front of the man holding my daughter, offering no explanation. We all then went upstairs to my room. Thinking back to the travails of Hattie's adoption that had caught me in a vise of contending ministries, I feared facing the legalities awaiting me. Several ladies then joined us with papers for me to sign. Mr. Pei guided me through the bureaucratic matters swiftly, never even requiring me to produce documents establishing my identity. With the papers gathered, the baby was handed to me matter-of-factly—patting me on the back, which touched my soul—and everyone filed out of the room except for Mr. Pei and an older woman, apparently a caregiver from the orphanage, who carefully sized me up and stroked the baby before slowly backing away. I delicately touched the woman's arm, assuring her in Chinese of the baby's well-being as my new daughter and thanking her. At first disoriented by suddenly hearing her own language coming from me, she flashed a broad smile, rubbed the baby's shins, and left. When I asked Mr. Pei about his earlier instruction of silence, he brushed aside my inquiry by simply snapping, "Politics!" As he was leaving, he assured me that we would be getting together often during my sojourn in Luoyang and instructed me to be downstairs in the lobby tomorrow at 8:30 a.m. That the procedure had been expeditious in no way shortened my prescribed stay. But unlike in Hangzhou, where bureaucratic stress had denied Myrna, Hattie, and me the opportunity to properly explore the scenic city, I looked forward to a pleasant time in my baby's hometown. I held my new fourteen-month-old daughter in my arms, her sweet smell weakening my knees. She then patted me again on the back.

This adoption was so very different from the first. Already a father and now in a hospitable environment, I was less anxious and able to pay more attention to my new daughter, a pudgy bairn already oozing indiscriminate charm—a survival technique, no doubt. I was not disarmed by the constancy of my girl's good cheer, though. I took it for what it was: a lack of discernment, prompting her to treat everyone in the same fashion. I welcomed the prospect of eventual bad temper, indicating emotional priorities. Now alone with Ottilie and whispering "Baby Tillie" in her ear, I dashed down the hall to find the others. We then returned to the room where the paperwork had been done. I changed the baby's diaper and put on the yellow dress that Iris had sent along for her; it was a mighty tight squeeze. Then, after eating a bit of mushy cereal, Tillie fell asleep, surrounded by loving admirers. When she awoke, I dug a parrot beanie baby out of my bag, which she immediately held close. When Marybeth commented that Tillie's gums seemed to be bothering her, I dug further in my bag, producing a Tiffany heart-shaped silver rattle. Tim and Marybeth then left me with my girl, whose radiance was almost too intense to behold.

Later that day we regrouped. Tim brought a bottle of champagne and a red plastic baby bathtub, sparing Tillie the intimidating tub in our room. Nonetheless, Tillie let her presence be known as we gently washed her and leisurely sipped champagne. We fed her again, dressed her in pink, then went downstairs to sample the local delicacies in the hotel's restaurant while she slept across my lap.

In the morning, Mr. Pei's driver arrived to take us to the ancient Longmen (Dragon Gate) Grottoes along the banks of the Yishui River, dating back to the end of the fifth century and elegantly lined with Buddhist statues and carved stones. As we strolled, ladies kept stopping to warn us sternly about the dangers of a chill and to ensure that the baby's legs were covered; they tugged at her leggings, which tended to rise up. I could not help but be struck by the endless concern and good wishes expressed when we chatted about our newly adopted little girl.

We had no appointments the next morning—the day before Easter—so we decided to take it easy. First we sent Hattie a fax from Tillie, saying how she was on the lookout for a pink tricycle up here in Luoyang, which she would be bringing home for her big sister. Tillie's entourage then took a stroll around the town, clearly a place of great civic pride. Yet more ladies fussed about the baby's exposed calves, and, wherever we turned, there were references to peonies, with bushes everywhere but not one bloom in sight. Along the way, the baby giggled as she nuzzled into my shoulder and pushed her face into my cheek. She clearly was enjoying being out on the town, very lively and responsive, always listening for sounds and following movements. With Tillie in my arms, I grew expansive, wanting to share her with Marybeth and Tim and acknowledge their feelings about having Tillie in their lives. By now, Julian's absence was palpable. Scheduled to arrive late on Easter Sunday, he had been apprehensive about leaving Hattie alone with Luna—not because of lingering anxiety about the baby having broken her leg on Luna's watch but because we would both be away welcoming her sister into the family.

The baby slept through the night, and so did I. The absence of stress, which had stalked us in Hangzhou, engendered calm. In the morning, when Tim took leave for Hong Kong, I caught sight of him staring yearningly at Tillie; I wished him fatherhood.

The ringing phone snapped me out of a reverie. It was Mr. Pei informing me that the paperwork was now done, warranting a celebratory *shuixi* (water feast), with its twenty-four courses, including many soups. He would pick me up at 5:00 p.m. in the lobby. "My treat," I volunteered. With Tim gone and Marybeth and Amy wanting to stay behind with Tillie, I was hoping Mr. Pei would bring along sidekicks to help with the sumptuous banquet and dilute the intensity of the evening, but no such luck. Of far greater importance, however, was his delivery of the baby's documents before we went to supper.

Later that night Julian finally arrived. He stood at the foot of the crib, staring at our sleeping daughter, and sang his own lyrics to "Cotton Blossom" by Jerome Kern, to which we had danced with Hattie before leaving Hong Kong:

Hello, Tillie. Hello, Tillie.
Hello, Tillie. How are you?
Hello, Tillie. Let's be silly.
Hello, silly Tillie.

The next morning the baby's sweet smile brought tears to Julian's eyes. No trip to a bird market or baby tumbling to a lobby floor was needed for the magic to take hold between this new father and Baby Tillie. Right before Mr. Pei's driver came to pick us up for an outing to the White Horse Temple, a fax arrived from Caritas, alerting us to an earlier slot at the Guangzhou US Consulate for final formalities. Since the adoption process had been so smooth, Tiffany wanted to get us back to Hong Kong earlier, but I was unsure if we would have the requisite medical report in time for an earlier interview. I expressed my concern, but she offered comforting assurances.

We were then off on our tourist excursion. En route, the driver told us about the White Horse Temple, the first Buddhist monastery built in China and still inhabited by monks. Often punctuating his spiel by mentioning the site's famed tranquility, the driver could not help but burst out laughing upon our arrival there. He had forgotten that it was Qing Ming, the festival during which families gather to clean ancestors' graves and mark the occasion with feasting. The ancient temple, a natural magnet for such gatherings, was bedlam—into which we happily ventured. Tillie was a star, attracting well-wishers who of course expressed anxiety about her legs. Many people also confided their delight that the baby was being adopted. Though touched, I was nonplussed; in a mere moment, a complex saga was suddenly whirling about me. Their child was now mine, taken from them and placed in my arms—by political edict. I couldn't decide if these kindly people were blind to their own world or casting me as a savior rescuing the baby from a world they saw only too clearly.

Back at the hotel, we stayed in for supper, feeding the baby in Marybeth's room. Sated, Tillie let fly a thunderous burp, causing us to howl. Julian and I then decided to call home. Hattie simply could not grasp that we were far away with her sister, but she homed in on the tricycle when we mentioned it, already hidden on the landing outside our front door. Exhausted by the day's outing and truly beholding our new baby, Julian fell fast asleep well before Tillie. As I then leisurely scrutinized the baby's Chinese passport, I discovered with sinking dread that Tillie's new surname had been omitted.

In the morning, I kept silent about the documentary glitch, which had grown more menacing during a sleepless night. After Julian, Marybeth, and the baby went off to the grottoes so Julian could see them with some company, I phoned Mr. Pei in a panic about the flawed passport. "She has so many names," he lamented, "we just ran out of space." Despite the hassles now awaiting him to address the omission, he assured me that the matter would be immediately corrected. He then confessed his confusion over foreign names, seeking my guidance to ensure that things were done right this time. We agreed on "Ottilie L. Beata Lighte," despite my guilt about omitting Julian's mother's name from the document; "Beata," shorter than "Lorraine," would fit.

When everyone returned gushing about the splendid grottoes and the baby's magnetism, I told them about the resolution of the passport mishap. Sensing my need for an outing and Julian's need for some respite, Marybeth asked me to come with her to buy souvenirs for her nieces and nephews. After wandering in and out of several stores, we realized that there was little without decorations of peonies, including paintings, embroidery, snuff bottles, and pottery. Once we gave up on finding alternative motifs, she swiftly made appropriate purchases. When we exited the taxi back at the hotel, Marybeth was holding Tillie in her arms. The slovenly driver was so taken with the baby that he motioned his desire to cuddle her. As I smiled and nodded in assent to his request, Marybeth recoiled from this disheveled man, wrapping her arms protectively around the baby. I tried to intercede, regarding her behavior as insensitive and a criticism of my parental judgment— as though I would knowingly endanger Tillie's health over the feelings of a driver. As Marybeth took flight with the baby, the best I could do was awkwardly declare, "I am a good father," a non sequitur that became a standing joke for the rest of the trip.

Back at the room, Mr. Pei called, suggesting that we take an outing to Xiyuan Park, where some blooming peonies had been sighted. Once there, we finally came upon two barely visible buds, allowing us to pronounce our mission accomplished, much to my relief. Upon our return to the hotel, a message at the front desk from Mr. Pei alerted us to the evening's plan: we were expected at a restaurant presided over by a nationally recognized dumpling chef named Mr. Kong Qingdong. Marybeth demurred, offering to babysit. As we sped off, it dawned on me that having Julian at my side had become perfectly natural to those around us, obviating the need for an explanation. In fact, his presence would have appeared conspicuous only if it had been explained. There seemed something particularly Chinese about the transformation of our alien situation into a scenario of no interest. Radio silence about homosexuality simply denied confusion; it did not deny us. I reckoned that if there was no chitchat about what Julian and I were rather than who we were, few would take heed.

We were greeted warmly again by the charming Mr. Pei and various colleagues. Immediately after handing me the baby's corrected passport, he let it be known that this was to be a celebratory send-off. Aside from the fact that I believed him to be a fine gentleman, I could not help but imagine the kind of pressure he had been subjected to by Mr. Xu to ensure that this adoption went off without a hitch.

We had a remarkable final feast. The dumplings were scrumptious, with countless fillings wrapped in exotic colored dough, inspiring awe. Not until the banquet was ending did Mr. Pei hail the emergence of Chef Kong from the kitchen, along with final platters of the world's tiniest handmade dumplings, for which Mr. Kong was globally renowned. In fact, I was told he often gave master classes on their preparation in Japan, the finest possible testimony to such obsessive-compulsive culinary skill. As he strode out in pristine whites, I sprang to my feet and delivered a few expected words of praise on behalf of our party. Since he shared Confucius's surname, I gushed that he was naturally wise and talented. Guessing that he was the sage's landsman from Shandong Province as well, where locals are known for their height, I commented on his imposing stature. Puffed up by my ingratiating and luckily informed comments, he launched into an oration on his career as a chef trained in Vienna and the honors heaped upon him over the years. The perky kitchen staff appeared and surrounded the chef, who seemed more like an Irish tenor than a renowned cook. Mr. Kong went on to finish his performance, with encores. Alongside the warmth I felt after so sweet an evening was incredulity; I felt halved between awe for Mr. Kong's mastery and for a performance right out of a Mel Brooks movie—guilty in the moment.

Back at the hotel we called Hattie, who was keen to sing "Twinkle, Twinkle, Little Star" and her ABCs to the baby. Since Tillie was fast asleep, we were obliged to falsely report that she had listened to the songs with delight.

Mr. Pei was on hand the next morning to see us off. It was difficult to leave this rare gentleman and Tillie's hometown, despite my eagerness to be away. After I had settled back in the car and happily unfocused as we left the city, the driver veered over to the shoulder of the road, having received an alert on his pager that a document had been forgotten—but nothing serious, we were assured. Gripped by that special brand of alarm I knew so well when advised that a bureaucratic "problem was not big," I visualized our convoy heading back to the hotel. But then a taxi roared up ahead of us, and its passenger rushed toward our car, handing me an envelope and explaining that it contained a receipt for the charitable donation I had made to the orphanage! Again on our way, it took almost an hour to get beyond the chaos of an accident. Then, when finally gliding along the highway, the driver quietly commented that there was a problem with the van carrying our luggage. On the side of the road once more, the two drivers stood over the van's exposed engine. Despite minimal mechanical knowledge, I divined that there was a leak in the radiator and started unloading the luggage. Finally, while the drivers continued their animated discussion, I managed to quietly shift everything, fitting more stuff in that car than basketball players into a Volkswagen. We then left the crippled van, its driver embarrassed about both the unresolved problem and his inability to see us off personally. We made it to the airport just in time for Julian and Marybeth to leave for Hong Kong. Amy, Baby Tillie, and I later headed for Guangzhou, where I would welcome her help in coping with its impenetrable Cantonese dialect.

It was pleasurably familiar to be back at the White Swan Hotel, with its procession of new families biding their time as they awaited final processing next door at the US Consulate. Once Tillie had settled in, I called home. Hattie was feeling upset, Luna mentioned.

Julian couldn't wait to recount an adventure he had had while en route to Hong Kong. "A randy Chinese pilot shamelessly hit on Marybeth! She rescued herself by draping her arm around my shoulder and introducing me as her husband. I now have not only a baby but a wife, as well," he roared. "I must ring off now," he suddenly declared, his mood changing on a dime.

In a moment, a new brand of parenting presented itself, requiring devotion to two children. It was not about splitting attention; instead, it was as though peripheral vision had been expanded, enabling us to scan the family landscape, mindful of it all rather than focusing on one member at a time.

With the baby in my arms, I went down to the dining room for supper. She was asleep even before I could put a napkin in my lap. But a leisurely meal never dawned on me. Soon back in the room, I tried calling Jeannette Chu, a pal from Hong Kong who was now the officer in charge of the local US Immigration and Naturalization Service. Keith, her husband, who also worked for the US government, told me that she was away on official business in Bangkok. Before my heart could sink, he assured me that his wife had already prepared a letter that was certain to ease our way when presented upon our arrival in America. He relayed only one bit of crucial advice from Jeannette: insist that the letter be read by the immigration officer before he so much as touches the baby's passport. One wrong stamp could derail her expeditious naturalization, thereby trapping her in America at the mercy of due process.

After an early breakfast, we presented ourselves at the US Consulate's medical office. All went smoothly, and I allowed myself a bit of parental swagger amongst the novices milling about with first children. We were then due for our exit interview with a Ms. Quistoff, who turned out to be a lovely woman. But that did not protect us from unforeseen impediments to final processing: the baby's Chinese passport, showing Ottilie L. Beata Lighte, did not match the adoption papers showing all four of the baby's names. It was also pointed out that Tillie had been categorized as "special needs"—Ms. Quistoff could not help but chuckle at this butterball in my lap being pronounced "malnourished"—and my home study had not qualified me to be the parent of a special needs child. I was first to contact Mr. Pei, who could attest to the fact that the computer's limitations made it impossible to provide all four names on the passport, and Amy was charged with calling Tiffany for appropriate Caritas documentation attesting to my fitness as the parent of a special needs child. After walking back to the hotel and asking Amy to take the baby for a while, I called Mr. Pei, who agreed to help us out. I then went downstairs for a Bloody Mary and a steak.

On our last scheduled day in Guangzhou, the puzzle was completed: Susan, our American lawyer, called me in the morning from Los Angeles to take my pulse; Mr. Pei confirmed that the message he had sent to the US Consulate had done the trick; and ditto from Tiffany. Shortly thereafter I received a message from the US Consulate requesting our presence at 3:00 that afternoon. At the appointed time, Jeannette's husband gave me a hug and handed me a letter addressed to the LA immigration authorities along with the baby's Chinese passport—now bearing an immaculately imprinted visa, enabling her to enter America. Once outside, I did a little dance with Tillie in my arms in the middle of the road, spinning so fast that centrifugal force almost caused me to lose hold of the baby, who giggled at the very moment that fear overtook me. We then drifted back into the hotel lobby, again circulating around the marble hall as though on a merry-go-round without horses.

The next morning I got up early with a sense of urgency about the journey to the airport, arriving so far ahead of schedule that we were able to get on an earlier flight. Immigration on both ends was uneventful, except for the admonition in Hong Kong that the baby must be gone in one week. The driver was there, having been alerted to the change of schedule. We first dropped Amy off and then headed home. Barely balancing the baby, luggage, and the long-hidden tricycle trimmed with pink ribbons while shouting, "Surprise," I opened our front door and saw only Julian, with no sign of Hattie.

My big moment having just fizzled, Hattie and Luna then awkwardly turned up right behind me. Hattie left the tricycle on its side and made a beeline for the baby. "Tellie," she squealed, sounding just like Luna, who had insisted upon the mispronunciation. After she helped feed Tillie, we all went downstairs and watched Hattie single-mindedly attempt a wobbly spin on her tricycle, her feet seeming to lengthen in order to willfully reach the pedals. As Hattie basked in the approval of her cheering parents, the sweet woman who looked after the building suddenly emerged, reacting to the unfamiliar hubbub. But upon seeing Hattie she burst out laughing and began babbling in Cantonese. Then, after spotting the new baby in Julian's arms, she melted in pleasure, asking if she could hold Tillie, whom we put in her arms.

The following morning Tillie started to make noises at around 5:00. We rushed in and grabbed her out of the crib to let Hattie sleep as late as possible. After feeding Tillie, we put her back to bed, where she slept until 9:30. However, our awkwardness about not yet having a rhythm for dealing with two daughters, coupled with the day's scheduled party celebrating Tillie's arrival, soon triggered Hattie's disquietude. As the day unfolded, no matter how many presents Hattie received or how much attention was lavished on her, she seemed to remain distant from Tillie, the interloper. In the course of the boisterous afternoon, I lost sight of Hattie and went looking for her. There she was, sitting on the floor beneath the window in her bedroom, staring at nothing, perhaps already recalling her days as an only child, now forever gone.

I gradually approached her. With the din of festivities left behind down the hallway, we were now all by ourselves. The pang that suddenly pierced me ironically was born of the very gift of empathy that Hattie herself had given me. Added to that was the guilt I was feeling over my complicity in her sadness, compounded by feelings of shameful disloyalty toward Tillie. I sat beside my girl and said nothing, taking cues from her about the way forward. She finally rose slowly and looked over her shoulder, inviting me to come along and face her new world beyond the bedroom door. Soon our friend Sandra, a glamorous screwball and gallery owner, enlivened Hattie by pretending to be sitting with her in a boat on the floor. Life further brightened when a cake appeared, celebrating Hattie's new role as a big sister as well as Tillie's arrival.

Once our guests had left, I called Mr. Xu to express my gratitude and ask if he would help Tillie obtain permission for an extended stay in Hong Kong, as he had done for Hattie. Again he graciously offered to wave his wand. He called back almost immediately, giving me the name of a contact who would be expecting us in Kowloon on Monday at 3:00 p.m. That evening our new family all got into bed and watched *Revelations*, Alvin Ailey's signature piece—as dear to me as a Rimsky opera was to Julian. Drawing me back to my own youth, when Alvin Ailey was just getting started and my mother was working at City Center, home to the young company, I sensed the four of us being woven not only together but into my past as well by the dancers leaping to that gospel music.

The next morning we went to see Dr. Pang for Tillie's checkup. At fourteen months, she weighed eighteen pounds and was sixty-six centimeters long, far more robust than Hattie had been when adopted at twenty months. Julian and I then escorted our new daughter to the Mandarin Coffee Shop for lunch, where she covered the floor beneath her high chair with bread that had started out in a basket on the table. Leaving a new carpet of starch behind us, Tillie and I parted from Julian in Central and took the ferry to Kowloon to sort out her visa extension in Hong Kong. Treated kindly and expeditiously by immigration authorities, courtesy of Mr. Xu, we were soon on our way back to Victoria Island, seated at the front of the ferry so Tillie could see the skyline, the breeze in our faces.

Back home, the four of us celebrated and danced to a vintage recording of Yvonne Printemps, the twittering chanteuse, who sang a ditty we mysteriously dubbed the "Malteser" song—though we could not fathom how its French lyric, "*Je t'aime quand même*," had morphed into the English confection by the same name. That it made no sense never diminished the song's ability to get us dancing with abandon. After collapsing into our massive Chesterfield sofa that evening, we fed and bathed the girls. Thinking back to our vigilance at bath time after Hattie's arrival, by comparison we seemed positively devil-may-care about washing our two little ones, now together in a place associated with joy rather than cleanliness. Then we read them stories and played the tape Julian had made for the nightly bedtime ritual, plying the girls with the likes of *Romeo and Juliet* by Prokofiev, Paul Robeson singing "Ma Curly-Headed Baby," and the Kronos Quartet playing a song from the album *Pieces of Africa*. Julian and I provided the finale, singing "I Know Where I'm Going" from our favorite film. As we left the room, we turned on the duck nightlight and stood in the doorway, marveling at our girls. Down the hall, Luna was awaiting us to recount that Hattie had told schoolmates, at great length, about her new tricycle but not a word about her new baby sister.

CHAPTER FOURTEEN

A Quartet at Last

Rejoice with your family in the beautiful land of life.
—ALBERT EINSTEIN

IT WAS SPRING, JUST BEFORE THE HEAT set in, and I relished paternity leave, though this period of time had yet to be identified in banking parlance. Tillie and I visited the women at Caritas, who swooned over her despite a particularly fragrant diaper. That Amy had been on both trips to China afforded her distinction, but I thought of Tiffany as the leading lady of my family's construction. After cookies, tea, and photographs, we were off to lunch with Christine, who had so lovingly chivvied me along the way; Tillie yet again flung bread about, to everyone's delight.

I was keen to get home before Hattie arrived from school so I could make a fuss over her. She bounded into the house along with Julian, who had again become a blond, as he had when Hattie was first settling in. Making the requisite noises that he might have been hoping for over the dye job, I was more than happy to acknowledge his need for attention as my partner rather than a family man.

With Tillie napping, Hattie had the full attention of her fathers, who pretended to be crocodiles, slithering around the sitting room floor trying to devour her. As playtime wound down, Tillie awoke. When I lifted her out of the crib, she peed on me, which I took as a sign of her disapproval for having been excluded from our hijinks in the swamp. That night in the bath Hattie noticed the baby's huge circular birthmark at the base of her spine that could have been mistaken for a bruise; in fact, most Chinese babies have this mark, which fades over time.

"You have one too, *Mein* Baby," I cooed, then sensed that my attempt at illustrating sisterhood was misfiring. To confirm the existence of *her* birthmark, I lifted her out of the tub so she could look at it in the mirror. After seeing it, she wanted to be returned to the bath, where she tried to explain the matter to Tillie. She stood before the baby, now called "mushface," likely derived from Hattie's pleasure at the word *mush* in the book *Goodnight Moon*, and proudly turned her bottom in Tillie's direction to show off her sisterly mark.

The best part of my new days came at their very beginnings. Always a morning person, I would pad into the girls' room and watch them as they slept and soon awakened. I didn't even mind changing diapers, much to Julian's relief. Then, with Julian and Luna up and about, I would happily recede, having already enjoyed my daily moments of magic. Hattie, of course, had strong opinions about what she would wear; she was drawn to intense colors, while Tillie's fair coloring seemed to call out for pale shades. Upon completing the parallel preparatory activities, we would all leave the house together and head for the tram, with Hattie dressed for school and Tillie in the red stroller. Luna and Hattie would then head up the Peak for a taxi, I would bear right to the station, and Julian would return home with Tillie. Julian's life as a composer had certainly been turned on its head, the demands and pleasures of our family leaving little room for anything but his gracious fatherhood.

This morning routine would not last much longer since we were soon preparing to leave Hong Kong for Los Angeles and the baby's naturalization. Meanwhile, world events had become personal when the Chinese Embassy in Belgrade was bombed by NATO planes, unleashing anti-American demonstrations throughout China. It was not inconceivable, I feared, that our plans could be derailed by political intrigue as the contending sides tried to extract themselves from the mishap. Ever since Hattie's place in our lives had been jeopardized by Hong Kong's return to China, world events never seemed far removed from me. Thus my anxiety had now been heightened by news from faraway Serbia. Even Mr. Xu phoned, wondering if the bombing had in fact been an accident. Chinese flags were lowered to half-staff in Hong Kong, and the bank issued a travel advisory for the mainland. With my concern about the baby's Chinese passport being stamped incorrectly upon our arrival in Los Angeles now tempered by dramas unfolding in China, I was greatly relieved that we would soon be departing for America.

On the flight to California, it did not take long for crew members and passengers to take notice of our family. It was fun to watch people walking down the aisle slow up as they tried to figure things out. Their unresolved curiosity, though, did not prevent them from being charmed by the girls as they slept, played, and ate. Christine, who was flying to America on business at the same time, had arranged to sit with us to help. She slept; the fathers didn't. Then, carrying the baby in a sling after we landed, I finally stood before the immigration officer, my voice calm as I placed the explanatory letter before him. He took great pains to assure me that the stamp about to be put in the Chinese passport was appropriate and would present no impediments to the baby's timely naturalization. But the customs agent further along could not figure out our family, with Julian and Christine each holding a baby as I fumbled with forms. When I handed them to her as we all moved as one while pushing luggage trolleys, she asked, "Who belongs to who?" to which Julian replied, "We all do. It's a new world." We spotted Cousin Billy, but Julian and I were at first too exhausted to appreciate his delight at seeing us. However, the loving hospitality that he and his wife, Patty—along with their own girls, Emily and Allie—were extending to our family dashed our torpor.

Upon our arrival at Billy's home, I needed to finalize arrangements for a celebration to be held after the baby's American passport had been obtained. Despite my usual reluctance to presume that procedures would be successful, I had allowed myself an ounce of confidence—without tempting the fates, I prayed. From afar, I had booked a faded mansion called The Palace, with wandering flamingoes and a pergola in its garden, where a klezmer band would be playing. Billy and Patty's home in Hancock Park quickly became Hattie and Tillie Central, with people appearing and gifts being delivered. The scene became all the sweeter as our girls took pleasure in playing with their new cousins; we were soon down there on the floor with the four little girls. Then Susan, our lawyer, called to share the good news that the baby's file had safely arrived in the Bell Flower office of the immigration authorities and that our appointment at this remote outpost was set for the following Tuesday.

We enjoyed random moments of pleasure while awaiting the day of the interview. Hattie went off with Billy and his family to Sabbath services, barely saying good-bye to us. When she finally returned after 9:00 p.m., Julian and I could only wonder how we would ever cope with her out on a date. On a shopping spree the next day, when Hattie was offered a choice of dolls, she declaratively picked Jackie Kennedy rather than the Virgin Mary or various Barbies; the foil for these vignettes was Tillie, whose noisy and lively disposition had only enhanced sisterly good cheer. I was also asked by my godson Jeffrey to show up at his school as a stand-in on Grandparents' Day, assured that no one would take me for an old man. I won the prize for having traveled the farthest to be part of the festivities and sat through endless presentations made bearable only by the smile on Jeff's face.

That evening Aunt Fran, in her incomprehensible Boston twang, regaled me with a tale of my parents' engagement in the late 1940s: along with lots of friends, the couple went out to see *A Streetcar Named Desire* to celebrate the occasion. Uncle Jerry drank so much during the supper party held afterward at the 21 Club that he had to be dumped into a taxi with a five dollar bill tucked into his breast pocket and sent home. There was no way to alert the chaps awaiting him at some unknown watering hole that he would be standing them up. Then, as powerful testimony to the miracle of our daughters, lots more friends and relatives began showing up, including Marybeth and Kathy, the two godmothers; Mark, who had been knighted by the Italians for his collection of paintings by Cesare Dandini, an obscure seventeenth-century artist—an obsession hardly expected of a Texan; Sue, our American friend from England who had recently moved to Los Angeles; Gary, an old pal from my days in Beijing; and Sandra, the madcap art dealer from Hong Kong who had once lifted Hattie's spirit in a pretend boat.

On the day of our arrival at the immigration office, it was obvious that we had been expected. The interview was brief; I swore an oath, signed a paper, and was told to wait half an hour for the paperwork to be completed. Susan happily held the baby as I marveled at the spadework she had done, ensuring so civilized an experience. Then suddenly I was called to the counter and, instead of being handed Tillie's certificate of citizenship, which would have permitted me to obtain her passport, was told that the photos submitted were the wrong size. My panic was instantaneous, setting in even before the clerk could help solve the problem by kindly directing me to a nearby photographer. The situation was readily corrected, and, with the certificate finally in hand, we drove back to Billy's home. But that evening, despite our success, things were kept low-key because we were not yet home free: there was still the matter of obtaining a passport.

Two days later we went to the Federal Building to pick it up. Aside from a long wait—like being in a surreal bakery having taken a very high number—all went according to plan. In fact, it was the pedestrian nature of the transaction that I actually found comforting. In short order, though, we were overtaken by frivolity and headed for Bloomingdale's, where our two-father family, still a rare sighting even on New York's Upper East Side, took the place by storm. It wasn't long before the makeup artists—they could have been transplanted from Manhattan—shed their affect and chirped over Hattie as she again romped on a checkerboard marble floor, much as she had done in Manhattan as a toddler. Tillie was asleep in my arms, missing the show.

By the time we arrived back at "headquarters," the house was filled with more well-wishers thrilled by our receipt of the passport, which was immediately passed amongst them for close inspection. Each guest was then handed a flute filled with champagne. Out on the veranda with Tillie in my lap and a drink in my hand, I greeted everyone, chattering about the happy outcome of the day.

The next day was devoted to a formal photo session planned by Patty, who had had four identical white linen dresses made for the girls to wear at the shoot. We dashed to Pasadena in our rented convertible. Julian, who usually liked to drive, felt uneasy navigating the roads on the right side, still very much the Brit. The girls were displeased as well, objecting to the glare in their eyes. When we finally arrived at the studio for an event that did not come naturally to us, its awkwardness was compounded by the stress of the journey. Now in their dresses, three of the little girls danced merrily about, allowing the canny photographer to capitalize on their good cheer. This kid whisperer was soon charming them into poses, even incorporating Tillie into the shoots. By the time Julian and I were asked to join them for family portraits, our disapproval of so stodgy an event had mellowed due to our regard for the photographer's way with children. En route back, no longer enchanted by surf culture, I swapped the convertible for a dreary sedan and did the driving. With the coming of babies, I was learning to cheerily part with my fanciful constructs, allowing them to evaporate in the glare of practicality. That evening we went to supper with other cousins. Two extremes marked the occasion: the beauty of the Blue Nile roses in the garden and the odor of Tillie's diaper, which led to a most unflattering nickname—Miss Landfill.

The day after was our big party. Patty and I left early to check out the arrangements at The Palace. We were greeted by its owner, Mrs. Nelson, a hospitable Nicaraguan woman, but the caterer had not yet arrived. Pacing in front of the house, we caught sight of his van down the road. When we went to investigate, we discovered that he had mistakenly gone to an address where another party was scheduled. When Patty and I were satisfied that plans were back on track, we returned to her house to get everyone ready. I immediately reported to Hattie that not only were there flamingos in the garden but swans as well, which Patty and I had spotted as we explored the property.

When we all arrived for the party, the Bucovina Klezmer Band was tuning up. Guests soon followed in droves—amongst them relatives barely known to me, along with friends of friends—all delighted to be part of our celebration. I was particularly happy to see my cousin Roy, the prototype for a character in *The Odd Couple;* Matt Meier, my old boss from the history department at the University of Santa Clara; and Thelda, a friend from Bronx Science days, now a physician in Kansas City. But it was a gentle dance with Julian—the babies in our arms, swaying in front of the pergola to the klezmer music, with guests enjoying themselves at a very different speed—that I still replay on a joyful mental loop.

The time had finally come for us to leave the sanctuary of Billy and Patty's home. To be sure, for their role in our lives they had joined the pantheon of dearest ones. My family had now been formed, with new adventures of everyday life awaiting us back in Hong Kong.

CHAPTER FIFTEEN

Lard in the Pews

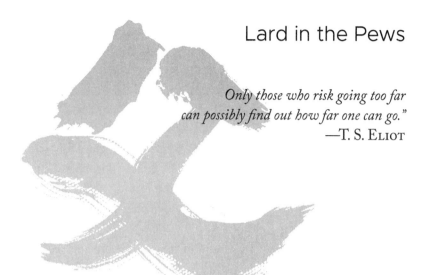

*Only those who risk going too far
can possibly find out how far one can go."*
—T. S. ELIOT

AFTER FINALLY LANDING IN HONG KONG following yet another exhausting flight, we sailed through immigration. Nestled in the arms of their English and American fathers, Hattie and Tillie, while Chinese, were now holding foreign passports and thus swiftly given leave to remain. Gobsmacked and humbled by the magic of reality, I was now living happily within my own dream.

That I was at ease with our new lives organically unfolding, however, did not mean that I was about to leave things to chance. In these days prior to civil partnership—let alone marriage—for gay citizens, I was obliged to focus on our girls' sense of place, ensuring that they be moored well in our family. It came as no surprise that deficient law could only be brought to bear indirectly through wills and passports. Our legal agreements at the time looked more like interlocking directorships of corporations domiciled in the Cayman Islands than a young family seeking sensible security. But there was more to security than documents. Music would soon become cultural epoxy, further strengthening our familial ties. Julian took us well beyond my Broadway chestnuts and "friend" Handel from Beijing days. His life of music became effortlessly ours, merrily ensnaring us in melodies and lyrics that soon formed our own very tuneful world. Beginning at the party in Hong Kong marking Hattie's arrival, when he produced percussion instruments for all the children and led them in performing, Julian established himself as our maestro-in-residence. We went on to dance to Massenet, hop on beds to Rimsky-Korsakov, and pantomime to Shirley Verrett. And then there were the public performances of his own compositions with the thrill of applause, a far cry from my lame calligraphy demonstrations at the dining room table that well outlasted the girls' attention spans. It was two little girls, though, who were binding us together.

In addition to music, my brand of religion became a presence in our lives, forging further family bonds. Since Julian was indifferent to matters of religion, he was relieved that it fell within my bailiwick. I had grown up in a cushioned version of Conservative Judaism, hardly feeling at all hemmed in by strict rules. We ate bacon, my mother paid religious fiddle-faddle no mind, my father was loath to even acknowledge his Judaism, Aunt Marcy had once snuck spare ribs into her kosher home to celebrate my passing an algebra exam, and Uncle Dave allowed us to watch television on Rosh Hashanah—if the Yankees were playing in the World Series.

But something more than Judaism's quirky charm had taken hold. Several months before my bar mitzvah, my mother had been hospitalized, agreeing to treatment only if she could attend the ceremony, and my father had sprinted from his brief third marriage, leaving me uncertain about whether he would show up. Testimony to the gloom of that day is my near-absence of memory; rather, when trying to recall the occasion I feel as though I am watching a silent movie featuring characters who move about without ever connecting; but that coarse woolen winter suit causing me embarrassment on the pulpit endures. A tarnished rite of passage, though, had not cut me off from Judaism's embrace. In fact, the religion's very survival in my life was testimony to its value as a lifeline through daunting times. I never even had to pray to be helped.

As my own family was forming, Judaism provided continuity with my family of origin and indicated what to do when I cared to pay attention, offering a bespoke framework of surety that served our needs. The ease with which my Judaism resurfaced did not surprise me. I was relieved to finally give up my wrestling match with religion. Many insist that they are not religious but are culturally Jewish. My brand of Judaism defied taxonomy and presented itself as a companion who knew just when to join me— no invitation necessary.

Upon returning with Hattie to Hong Kong, I wanted her named in a synagogue. Although I was drawn to the colonial charm of Ohel Leah, the Orthodox congregation named for the matriarch of the Sassoon family, as a gay father of an adopted Chinese daughter in a relationship with a non-Jew I would have been banished even before finishing my introduction to the rabbi. That left the United Jewish Congregation, the catchall for the non-Orthodox community. After making an appointment with its rabbi, I went to its location in a nondescript high-rise on Robinson Road. Upon entry, I was immediately put off, thinking it was yet another Reform synagogue that looked more like a Danish motel than a house of worship. Things only got worse when I heard folk singing and guitar strumming, a far cry from the choir singing and organ playing in Temple Adath Israel in New York City that had shaped my sense of how Jewish services should look and sound. But then, as though remotely sensing that if left on my own for another moment I might flee, Rabbi Oseran suddenly emerged to offer a warm welcome and usher me into his office. Putting me at ease so quickly that my own formality seemed ridiculous, he was unfazed about the way forward, without any hint that a rite of passage for the child of a two-father family would not be possible. I felt like grabbing his hands and doing a hora on the spot but realized that such a display of Ashkenazi exuberance would not have worked. Instead, I hugged him.

For the very reason I had found Reform Judaism annoying—that it stood for nothing/everything—Hattie's naming ceremony now seemed possible without objection from the clergy. Soon we were dealing with the mundane logistics of planning the event, focusing on catering, and bringing Julian and the baby in to meet the rabbi and discuss how events would unfold. From the outset of our chat, with Hattie scampering about, it was clear that the rabbi regarded our girl as a pure and gentle being whose welcome into Judaism was an honor and a joy. His concern seemed to be that our family, headed by pioneering gay fathers, be represented in fitting fashion within a religious context. The rabbi was not interested in insurrection. Rather, his view was that I simply wanted to bring my baby to join me within the fold. As the Jewish parent, I was assigned the heavy lifting during the dogma-lite ceremony, and Julian was to join me on the pulpit to hold our girl high as she was embraced by Judaism, followed by immediately welcoming up honored guests.

On the evening of the event, before a packed sanctuary charged with goodwill, the ceremony ran its course so smoothly that it could have been forgotten that our singular family was still very much on the cultural and political barricades. There was one surprise, though: its impact on Julian. Unlike me, he had no religious guide as a child—or the predictable good smells that came out of Aunt Marcy's kitchen on holidays. That he now had a family being publicly sanctified came as a shock to him. On that evening, we watched him get lassoed by the power of belonging. And, for presiding over this transformational event with masterful good cheer, Rabbi Oseran was promoted to champion of our two-father multiethnic family.

Not long afterward, when it became clear that Tillie would be joining our family, it seemed natural to enlist Rabbi Oseran to preside over her naming ceremony as well. For the appointment to discuss this, I swaggered into the synagogue, so unlike that first visit when I had been irked by the place and apprehensive about how our family would be viewed. In addition to arranging for Tillie's ceremony, I wanted to discuss rumors that the rabbi had encountered disapproval amongst the Orthodox community for his involvement in Hattie's ceremony. When I brought up my concern, he offhandedly alluded to a bit of bother, skating over the matter, keen only to hear about the new baby. But then he expressed regret that Tillie's ceremony would not be taking place on his watch because his stint in Hong Kong was drawing to a close; thus the privilege would fall to his successor, who, he assured me, would welcome Tillie with open arms.

When Rabbi Oseran's successor arrived, I went to discuss arrangements regarding our second rite of passage. The new rabbi, a scrappy Australian, immediately put me at ease about the matter but also recounted the travails of his predecessor. "Good job that the first ceremony was not down to me, mate. Sure dodged a bullet on that one," he commented. I asked why, having only been exposed to his predecessor's joy as Hattie's ceremony unfolded.

"Sounds like you don't know what went on, Peter," he continued, his good cheer immediately displaced by a serious demeanor. "That bloody Orthodox zealot crucified Rabbi Oseran after Hattie's ceremony. A smear campaign was waged against a man who simply wanted to bless your little girl."

As tears streamed down my cheeks, the new rabbi placed his hand on my shoulder, assuring me that he would do right by Tillie. "Just let me do my job, and bring the fuckers on," he firmly instructed, letting slip a smile. As if to emphasize our place in the flock, he then mentioned that a French photographer named Frédéric Brenner would be coming to Hong Kong to document the Jewish community. In keeping with my abiding desire to weave our family into a larger world, I expressed interest in our being included in the record. The rabbi said that the photographer's visit would be overseen by the Orthodox community but assured me that all Jews would be included, which left me wary. Aware of my hesitation, he then made it clear that precisely because of my discomfort our family was all the more obliged to show up for the photo shoot and be counted. At that moment, my Uncle Jesse's mantra came to mind: "Keep your eye on the doughnut and not on the hole." I placed my name on the list.

I was soon notified that to participate in the photo shoot we would be required to wear red Mao jackets—the color that looks best in black and white photos—which could be ordered from a designated Shanghainese tailor. When I went to pick up our jackets, suddenly a sense of disquiet overtook me about the potential disapproval of my family by the Orthodox community. I had thought about writing to the rabbi who had attacked Rabbi Oseran for performing Hattie's ceremony but suspected my words would only be dismissed, and I did not want to confront him, fearing that I might either sob or grow violent. So I planned an act of spite. One evening I climbed the steep path to the summit of The Peak, went into Park 'n' Shop, and searched for a big box of individually wrapped packets of biscuits. After checking to be sure they included lard, a nonkosher cooking fat, I purchased them and returned home.

On the day of the photo shoot, I piled into the taxi juggling Hattie with her cast, the baby bag, the box of biscuits, the red jackets, and a framed picture of Tillie, who was still in Luoyang. Once at Ohel Leah, called "Jew Club" by the driver when given the address in my hopeless Cantonese, I located Nigel, an English barrister, and his daughter Hannah, and Ali, an English entrepreneur, and her daughter Grace—dear friends who gathered at our flat each Sunday, where the girls became competing fairies bouncing on beds. After getting the children into their red jackets, I asked Nigel and Ali if they would look after Hattie for a few moments, grabbed the bag of biscuits, and left. In the deserted synagogue, I separated the biscuit packages and secreted these *traif* souvenirs beneath the benches and in shelves holding prayer books along the pews. Having swiftly attended to my subversion in the sanctuary, I rejoined our group at the photo shoot.

The photographer was theatrically barking instructions, ensuring artful placement of participants along the facade on all levels of the building. Our group occupied a fine niche on one of the terraces, where, cradling Hattie, I held Tillie's photograph high in my free hand.

When the photo shoot was over, we all agreed to meet at our flat on Barker Road. On the taxi ride home, I took pleasure in mulling over my act of treason, realizing, though, that lingering respect must have prevented my opening the individual biscuit packets of revenge. Then the liberal New Yorker in me reared up with sudden awareness that I had placed the biscuits of defiance only upstairs, where women, other victims of Orthodox Judaism, were penned in by their menfolk.

Before long, that photo in a frame became a baby in my arms. With Hattie having paved Tillie's way, it was comforting for Julian and me not to be trailblazers for once. As promised, the new rabbi presented himself, more than ready to plan the naming ceremony. He indeed did his job, insisting that Julian and I stand together on the pulpit, holding the baby between us. That Hattie was weaving in and out of our legs only served to lend splendid ordinariness to religious pageantry. Our family was now beheld in crisp relief, all before a house packed with people who wanted to be part of a *simcha*, well within tradition and in front of it, as well. Julian and I lifted our pudgy girl high above us, and the congregation erupted in applause.

CHAPTER SIXTEEN

Heroines of the Torah

Every day is a journey, and the journey itself is home.

—BASHO

THE GIRLS' ADOPTIONS AND MY periodic job relocations demanded vigilance against discontinuity. But though our household was one of ritual it was not one of rule, the shape of our lives being firm yet sufficiently elastic to allow for creativity and spontaneity. Whether it was eating together, singing before bedtime, making up stories about Ferdie the ant, or pretending to reach for clouds on evening walks in a Japanese park, our ever-changing lives were moored in a portable rhythm that helped us transplant our roots to each new home. Another significant stake was put in the ground after we visited our friend Christine during the summer of 2001 on Shelter Island and subsequently returned every summer since. This bucolic haven added to the stability of our shifting lives. Kate, Christine's daughter and Hattie's best friend in Hong Kong, along with Tillie attended Camp Quinipet each morning. Then each afternoon at 4:00—with the sun gentler in the lower sky—we headed for Menhaden Beach, with its fine sand and vistas out to the sea beyond Bug Lighthouse and Gardiners Island. On his first visit there with the girls, Julian had been fortunate to meet up with a formidable academic who sported fire engine-red lipstick, the redoubtable Ann—Dr. Brunswick, to the masses. She had been readily charmed by Hattie and Tillie then had perked up after inquiring about Julian's wife and being told that he did not have one but rather a partner named Peter. It was through Ann that we were introduced to a group of friends who have remained steadfast for decades, each summer to be found on that beach at 4:00 p.m., with graduations, weddings, and funerals strewn along the way.

No matter where we were in the world, we returned to Shelter Island every summer, first to a rental in Shell Beach and then to a house we bought in Hay Beach, a ten-minute bicycle ride from the water. The constancy of our annual routine posed only one problem: with friends and family clamoring to see the girls, we were torn between our idyll and off-island obligations. We finally decided that upon arrival in New York each June from our foreign posting, before settling on Shelter Island we would host a party in the city, making it clear that if fans wanted to see the girls they could do so only at a watering hole called East of Eighth on West 23rd Street or on Shelter Island, thus beginning a decade-long ritual during which Hattie's and Tillie's annual blossoming charmed our guests. At these parties, there was always live music and varied fare, with each year's event tweaked just enough to keep the tradition fresh. Even Christmas came out of season, as the girls customarily received summertime gifts.

Significant scaffolding was rising around our lives, reminding me of photos I had seen of the Statue of Liberty's construction: the girls had been welcomed into Judaism and surrounded by music; they knew they could always weave between their fathers for support when they lost their bearings; and summers were always spent on Shelter Island amongst family and friends. By the time we moved to London from Tokyo in 2002, it only seemed natural for the girls to carry on with religious education, seeing them beyond infant ceremonies and potato pancakes. Thus I dutifully compiled a list of synagogues with Sunday schools, some of which were held on Saturdays. Since the categories of Orthodox, Conservative, and Reform lacked significance in England, I was guided by description rather than labels as I investigated potential schools. After passing up a rabbi who tried to impress me with outlandish street cred—"My doctor, who attends the orthopedic needs of the Queen Mother, is a transsexual"—we found a home at a synagogue opposite Lord's Cricket Ground in St. John's Wood. Once the girls had started their routine of attending weekly religious instruction, I puzzled them by sharing their annoyance at having to show up, telling them they were not supposed to like it, nor had I. Experiencing awkward kinship with the congregation, we became reluctant yet sincere regulars at the Liberal Jewish Synagogue.

I learned early on that in my family it was easier to address Judaism than matters Chinese. Upon Hattie's arrival in Hong Kong, I had slavishly spoken Chinese to her since she had come from Hangzhou and had heard the language for quite a while. It took about six months for me to surrender. Not living in a Mandarin-speaking environment—Cantonese is spoken in Hong Kong, and both Julian and our nanny only spoke English at home— Hattie came to regard me as a linguistic outlier, nevertheless allowing me to read her Chinese bedtime stories. Thus by the time Tillie arrived little Chinese was heard in our household, save those same stories featuring animal noises. Ultimately, I came to realize that success in imparting the language to the girls mattered less than my interest in Chinese on their behalf. I watched my friends wrestle with the Chinese heritage of their adopted daughters, ditching the true past only to replace it with a false one. Whether Hattie and Tillie spoke Chinese or not, their homegrown culture would always be in the ether of our family, courtesy of my obsession with China. It would always be there for them to grab as they saw fit. It was life itself that took care of my linguistic concerns. After we moved to Beijing in 2007, when the girls were nine and eleven, I put the word out for a housekeeper who spoke no English. Enter Xiao Wang, a delightful woman from Baoding, a city southwest of Beijing, who made the best dumplings ever—from scratch! The girls took to her immediately, and soon I was overhearing Chinese chitchat in the kitchen.

My determination to fortify our family's web of well-being remained constant. Along with arranging for the girls' education in Chinese, I again sought out a Jewish community, albeit sparse, to ensure some constancy in our disordered lives. I discovered a congregation too small to be fragmented by sectarian nonsense, with a delightfully motley flock of children being casually educated in a house located inside a curious gated community near the airport. I was soon envisioning bas mitzvah festivities for Hattie.

Ultimately, it was good fortune born of natural catastrophe that assured Hattie's next rite of passage. In the aftermath of the 2008 Sichuan earthquake, the foreign community banded together to raise money for relief efforts. Julian contributed a musical composition for an auction, which was won by a young journalist named Alison Klayman. Aside from her pleasing personality, professional accomplishments, and candidacy for our little girls' role model, she was a well-educated Jewess. By the time Julian had produced *Heroines of the Torah*—prompted by Alison's request that the title allude to powerful women—we had all become fast friends, and she had agreed to prepare Hattie for her bas mitzvah. As the event began to take shape, I alerted Rabbi Oseran, now back in Israel, to our plan, inviting the man who had named Hattie in Hong Kong to conduct the ceremony, mindful of keeping my family within a loving continuum.

During these preparations, just as I had not been deterred from fatherhood by an unhappy upbringing, I was able to revisit my own bar mitzvah, an event that had been assailed by unhappiness. Becoming a father had given me the courage to understand that history need not repeat itself. It was as though I now had a map to guide me safely through an obstacle course. I was able to ensure that my own unhappy occasion did not taint the present, allowing me to push ahead with arranging Hattie's ceremony.

Hattie was indifferent when it came to her outfit for the big day. Thus it did not take long for Julian and me to realize that we needed to outsource this project to our friend Lisa. I had known her since my first stint in Beijing during the 1980s, and now we were colleagues. It was her particular brand of warm yet unsentimental concern that got Hattie to show up at the dressmaker in Ya Xiu Market, Beijing's celebrated all-purpose emporium. Under Lisa's laissez-faire but watchful eye, Hattie chose a traditional fitted silver and black brocade *qipao* and jacket that served to illustrate the intent of the occasion; she was taking tentative steps toward womanhood. Then there were Hattie's practice sessions with Alison. Coaxing Hattie to make herself heard was as tough as getting her to choose a dress. Though she knew her portion cold, I would sometimes find them in a standoff at opposite ends of our sitting room—Alison, with cupped hand to her ear, cajoling Hattie to project her Hebrew murmurs toward her.

By the time the big day arrived, Hattie could indeed be heard chanting her haftarah portion and delivering a speech during which she deviated from her text by declaring that "eating pork does not make you a bad person." On that frigid February day in 2009, beyond Wangfujing, the broad shopping street, and a block westward of the Forbidden City, a real klezmer band, miraculously discovered by Julian, welcomed our guests, many of them from abroad, to the elegant venue Tiandi Yijia. Once an imperial storehouse with a Ming courtyard, the building was now covered in glass with white parasols hanging from the ceiling, its second floor converted into a synagogue for our event. Luncheon festivities were held on the floor below, where tables had been set up amidst an elegant grid of watercourses with koi swimming beneath us. We could not help but wonder which child would fall in first. None did! The high point of the traditional performances during the afternoon was face-changing by a master of Sichuan opera. So quickly did he switch his masks that no matter how closely one watched, his sleights of hand were impossible to detect. The next day we took Hattie and her friends to a restaurant where they could make noodles and dumplings from scratch—a successful event, judging by the amount of flour in each child's hair when it was over.

Soon after Hattie's triumphant occasion Julian and I decided to leave for America when it was time for her to attend high school. Since we did not want to stay in Beijing till her graduation or interrupt her subsequent schooling, this way forward seemed prudent. We also then realized that Tillie's bas mitzvah would then be held amongst strangers in Princeton, where our new home awaited us. However, after doing some research I discovered that girls were eligible for their big day at age twelve rather than thirteen, as customary for boys. Thus, Tillie, too, could have her bas mitzvah in Beijing.

Although the girls were both born in February—two years apart—we agreed that another winter bas mitzvah was out of the question, opting instead for springtime festivities. But, aside from signing Alison on as Tillie's tutor and inviting Rabbi Oseran back for a return engagement, we did not want to simply repeat the activities of Hattie's bas mitzvah, which presented a challenging predicament.

I happened to bump into Juan van Vesselhove, a former Belgian banking colleague, who mentioned his involvement in a restoration project off the northeast corner of the Forbidden City. I discovered that the eighteenth-century Zhi Zhu Temple featured on Juan's card had been built on the grounds of an even older sutra printing shop, establishing the site's bona fide Buddhist connection. Enchanted by the prospect of Tillie's celebration being held in a place vibrating with such history, I called Juan and booked the venue site unseen, assured that there was enough time to prepare the space.

Once we had returned from Shelter Island at the end of the summer, our departure from Beijing, though a school year away, was quickly approaching, and Tillie's upcoming bas mitzvah in April, not far off. As preparations began, she, unlike her sister, couldn't wait to sprint to the local seamstress. Tillie opted for the Audrey Hepburn look of simple color blocks in silk. Julian arranged a concert for guests the Thursday prior to Tillie's ceremony, and we were pleasantly surprised that many out-of-town people joined us. Tillie took delight in the fact that sixty guests from abroad, twenty more than had shown up for her sister's bas mitzvah, were attending—to which Hattie riposted, "Mine was in February. What do you expect?"

After finally being given the all-clear by Juan, Julian and I visited the venue two days before Tillie's bas mitzvah. The clouds were low with an unseasonably wintry chill in the air as we struggled to find the place. Once within the temple precinct behind a rusted, groaning doorway, we stood in mud, with an exposed septic tank blocking our way. Juan was soon rushing toward us, his effusive warmth and outsized grin doing little to put us at ease. Assuring us that an army of workers was on call to submerge the tank by Saturday morning, he hurried us into the temple with its forest of massive red pillars, distracting us from a construction site mere feet away. Our feeling of awe as our eyes swept upward to the roof supported by the grove of vermilion columns temporarily relieved our anxiety. We then visited a nearby modern building, where a luncheon of French fare would be served. Since the facility did not have a Chinese kitchen that could accommodate our group, we had hired a caterer from a continental bistro offering scrumptious food. Reassured by Juan and the elegant vestiges of history that our event could be successful, we beat a hasty retreat, hoping for the best.

On the morning of the bas mitzvah, the sun shone, and the septic tank, as promised, was nowhere to be seen. We were greeted by a country and western band, coached by Julian in the klezmer style—a group looking more like the Village People than Ashkenazi music-makers. The temple's impressive interior did little to keep our guests warm despite the calendar saying it was springtime. But there Tillie stood, an electrifying waif of a kid, managing to enliven Leviticus with a voice oozing moxie, her sound soaring high within the reborn house of worship.

With Tillie's bas mitzvah behind us, we departed from Beijing. First we headed for Shelter Island with a new addition, Fuqi, our precious mutt found as a two-week-old puppy abandoned in a box near a Beijing lake. Then, at summer's end, our itinerant brood finally arrived at our Princeton cinder block house where I had been a cat sitter as a student, a stone's throw from the Graduate College, my residence while studying China's past. We had now come to a halt after wandering the world, but there was no bathos in our stillness. I realized that we had long been at home, ever since finding one another along the Way.

EPILOGUE

There is a labyrinth which is a straight line.
—Jorge Luis Borges

After jumping into the chilly and choppy sea, I clumsily defogged my goggles and adjusted my snorkel while treading water. With flippers and arms finally in synch, I set off on a swim of discovery. I quickly found myself hovering above a carpet of huge and aged turtles arrayed on the seafloor beneath me. I tried to count them but quickly surrendered to wonderment. Then, blindsided by one of the enormous animals brushing up against me, I behaved like other animals at home in the Galápagos Islands. Fear simply did not dawn on me; it was as though I had no predators.

Suddenly, something caught my eye off to the right, beyond the border of the turtle carpet where the seabed fell away. It was Hattie, who is most at home in the water, diving steeply alongside a sea lion, only to be cut off by a shark in purposeful transit. My fleeting panic subsided only after imagining that their mutual respect was keeping them out of each other's way. I was then startled by a tap on the shoulder. It was Tillie, initially skittish about snorkeling but now giggling as she taunted me about my clumsiness in the water before swimming off.

Hours later Julian and I sipped drinks in the ship's salon. After endless showers, the girls joined us to rehash the delights of the day. I sat back, very much the paterfamilias celebrating my seventieth birthday here in the Galápagos; yet, even after more than two decades of fatherhood, I was anything but complacent, still atingle with the excitement of having become a parent. Young women were now gabbling beside me, but they always seemed to have just miraculously arrived.

Holding those two babies in my arms for the first time at the tail end of the twentieth century was anything but inevitable. After all, mine had not been a life hurtling purposefully through time. A childhood cut short by parental divorce and a fraught upbringing, an obsession with China that marked my studies and career, an understanding of my homosexuality while at Princeton, and finding Julian had all led me on myriad detours that became my path. As a result, my becoming a father was thwarted neither by society's barriers to my sexual orientation nor by an itinerant career that took me far and wide around the world. In fact, it was susceptibility to distraction and adventure that saw me to fatherhood. There was no way to have prepared myself for the dramas that seemed to conspire, pushing children beyond my grasp; and it took more than an iron will to fuel a spirit enabling me to outrun that receding horizon. Had bloody-mindedness not been leavened by upbringing, education, escapades, romance, and Julian, I just might never have become the first single father in Hong Kong to have adopted children from mainland China.

Fatherhood became the backdrop before which we lived our lives; and fatherhood endures. Even my career seemed fleeting by comparison. After thirty-four years in banking, my swan song as J. P. Morgan's resident China hand, at the beck and call of global clients, faded naturally. Then, well-sprung into retirement, I was soon spending chunks of time in my Eames chair doing needlepoint—my version of two-dimensional mosaics—using the rowing machine at Dillon Gym, taking long swims off Shelter Island, riding my bicycle, doing some board work, and sauntering about.

One glorious afternoon not long after settling into my new routine I headed for Jones Hall to attend a lecture honoring F. W. Mote. I went past the Graduate College, where I gazed way up at my old room in Pyne Tower. Then, as I finally neared the East Asian Studies department, I caught a glimpse of the Woodrow

Wilson School and suddenly halted. Even before I sussed out the unexplained pause, a smile came to my face; Mr. Xu was paying my memory a visit.

Although he certainly had never faded from my consciousness, Mr. Xu's Princeton appointment as a visiting scholar right after his retirement from government had slipped my mind. In cahoots with a professor, I had stealthily arranged for an honorary position acknowledging his public service and my private esteem. Despite his thrill at such recognition and the pleasure I took in making it happen, ours had become an imbalanced relationship. While my gratitude for his part in the creation of my family never dwindled, he was more than happy to have traded his role as our miracle worker for simply being a presence well woven through our lives. In this moment, though, I felt that we were sharing the university side by side, defying the good sense of time.

Of all places, it was on Route 1 in New Jersey that I grasped the connection between Jung's concept of synchronicity—events meaningfully fastened together with no sensible links—and my own sense of time, more collage-like than sequential. One day as I was bound for Newark Airport to meet my elder daughter after her six-month sojourn in Japan, I suddenly recalled an old historical guide, *Imperial Rome to the Present Day*, which cannily illustrated the establishment of structures in ancient cities with transparent cutouts through which each sheet above revealed parts of the page beneath, bringing to life the evolution of architectural development. Then abruptly images of my daughters appeared in my mind, playing peekaboo through layered memories—grown up but somehow still toddlers—affording me the gift of experiencing events simultaneously as collages rather than sequentially. I realized that the story of my progress to parenthood was also like that guide to Rome, with new epochs superimposed on older ones, revealing aspects of each. Fatherhood for me was not only a stage in a sequential life. I knew that when I became a parent I had been given a chance to enjoy a sweeter version of my childhood while concurrently living through its later phases, experiencing how children are unique in their ability to allow adults to relive past chunks of time. On Route 1, time became plural and layered, with bits and pieces of memories jostling for screen time before me.

My days now are fashioned by both happenstance and purpose, revealing patterns both pedestrian and remarkable, with the miracles of fatherhood—our daughters now in their twenties—crafting their own times. Julian and I are upstage, very much part of their scenery, just where we belong.

ABOUT THE AUTHOR

Over his lifetime, Peter Rupert Lighte immersed himself in matters Chinese, all the while longing to become a father. After obtaining a PhD from Princeton in East Asian Studies, he haphazardly accepted a position at a bank that sought to mold him into a "renaissance banker." In 1982, he was dispatched to Beijing, which was then gradually emerging from the Cultural Revolution, to become a pioneering circuit rider traveling around a country he had come to know through Confucius and Ming gazetteers. Before long, he was briefing the US Secretary of the Treasury for a speech at the Great Hall of the People, explaining the significance of turkey to Premier Zhao Ziyang at President Reagan's Thanksgiving banquet, and having a bouquet of flowers brusquely snatched from his arms by the Australian prime minister to present to a Chinese dignitary.

After three years in Beijing, Lighte was posted to London, where he met his life partner, Julian Grant, a composer. Though resolved to become a father, he was at first thwarted by his sexuality and local authorities turning a deaf ear, obliging him to put his parental agenda on hold until the couple relocated to Hong Kong on the cusp of the colony's return to China in 1997.

Subsequently, the couple adopted two daughters from China, after which their family went on to Tokyo, London, and Beijing, where Lighte became the founding chairman of J. P. Morgan Chase Bank China. He now lives in Princeton, New Jersey, with his husband, Julian, and Fuqi, a mutt from Beijing. Their daughters, both Barnard women, are well out in the world. He is also the author of *Pieces of China* and *Host of Memories: Tales of Inevitable Happenstance*.